The Ultimate Canadian
Sports Trivia Book

The Ultimate Canadian Sports Trivia Book

Edward Zawadzki

Foreword by George Chuvalo

A HOUNSLOW BOOK
A MEMBER OF THE DUNDURN GROUP
TORONTO › OXFORD

Publisher: Anthony Hawke
Editor: Barry Jowett
Copy-editor: Natalie Barrington
Design: Bruna Brunelli
Printer: Webcom

Canadian Cataloguing in Publication Data

Zawadzki, Edward
The ultimate Canadian sports trivia book

ISBN 0-88882-237-5

1. Sports — Canada — History — Miscellanea. I. Title

GV585.Z39 2001   796'0971   C2001-901942-4

2   3   4   5   05   04   03   02   01

We acknowledge the support of the **Canada Council for the Arts** and the **Ontario Arts Council** for our pub-lishing program. We also acknowledge the financial support of the **Government of Canada** through the **Book Publishing Industry Development Program** and **The Association for the Export of Canadian Books**, and the **Government of Ontario** through the **Ontario Book Publishers Tax Credit** program.

                                                                    J. Kirk Howard, President

All images courtesy of Canadian Sports Hall of Fame. Except page 174 courtesy of The Twin Dragons, page 190 courtesy of Brian Budd, and page 217 courtesy of Edward Zawadzki.

Printed and bound in Canada.⊕
Printed on recycled paper.
www.dundurn.com

Dundurn Press
8 Market Street
Suite 200
Toronto, Ontario, Canada
M5E 1M6

Dundurn Press
73 Lime Walk
Headington, Oxford,
England
OX3 7AD

Dundurn Press
2250 Military Road
Tonawanda NY
U.S.A. 14150

This book is dedicated to the two best friends I've ever had.

My mom, Wanda — who selflessly gave all of us so much, including her great love of books. She constantly amazes me with her ability to love us, especially during those times that we don't deserve it. I suppose that's why they call it a Mother's Love. She's the one who should be the real writer in the family.

My late dad, Walter — who handed down to me his genuine love of all sports, especially boxing. His love of laughter rubbed off on me and his smile stays in my heart daily. My most precious memories of my pops are of us watching the fights together. (I can't wait to tell him someday what it was like to hang with Ali.)

And to Rebecca and her trusty computer. You definitely deserve a raise.

TABLE OF CONTENTS

ACKNOWLEDGEMENTS

Much love and thanks to:

Allan Stewart and the staff of the Canadian Sports Hall of Fame.
"You are the keepers of the Torch"
"The Protectors of the Flame"
Many thanks for all your help.

My brothers Richard and George, and my niece Jessica, who I love
and give thanks for daily.

My late "Uncle" Ernie Fedoryn who never lost faith in me.

Judy McLeod, of the gutsy *Toronto Free Press*, who was the first to
inform me of the then-unknown fact that I was a writer.

Georgie C., who always motivated me and told me not to procras-
tinate, but to go out and do it. Advice that's worth millions, pal.
Will you take a post-dated cheque?

And my editor Barry Jowett, without whom this book wouldn't
have existed, and I'd still be fighting to be published.

FOREWORD

BY GEORGE CHUVALO

The Ultimate Canadian Sports Trivia Book is a must read for all sports aficionados. Read this book and become an instant Einstein on Canadian sports trivia. Even some of the up-to-now little-known boxing facts opened up my eyes.

Big Eddie has done more research than the F.B.I. The book has all the boss answers to all the boss questions.

If an acquainted reader should find themselves on *Who Wants to Be a Millionaire* and the subject of Canadian sports should come up, they will be a lead pipe cinch to go home with more than just a little loose change.

Introduction

When my partners and I in this literary undertaking — my partners being Dundurn Press — decided unanimously to go full steam ahead with this project, I have to tell you the truth: I was a little nervous I might run out of enough interesting stories, stats, and controversies to warrant a project of this considerable undertaking. There was no doubt that we could fill an entire library with just Canadian hockey trivia, but we wanted a diverse cross-section of all popular sports and competitors, and I thought I would have trouble finding a book's worth of material. When I began doing the serious research I realized just how wrong I was. As a sportswriter, broadcaster, and certified sports nut I'm a little embarrassed about how little I knew of our rich history in sports.

The stories are all here: the triumphs, the controversies, and the cast of talented athletes from all parts of our fair land, competing nationally and around the globe.

I truly hope that this book will not only inform, but entertain the reader as much as it did the author. I wish I could have learned this much in school.

BASEBALL

1. What city by-laws had to be amended before the Blue Jays could play in Toronto?

A. In pre-1977 Toronto it was illegal to stage any kind of sporting event on city property on Sundays. Toronto Council had to amend that ordinance to allow Sunday games, though for the first several years no games were allowed to start before 1:30 p.m.

2. Did Sparky Anderson ever play baseball in Canada?

A. Canada was very good to Sparky when his playing career was almost over. He came up here to play second base for the old Toronto Maple Leafs of the International League in 1960. By 1964, he was managing the club, and so impressed the boys in the big leagues that by 1969 he was managing the Cincinnati Reds.

3. Who is the only Canadian in the Baseball Hall of Fame?

A. Ferguson Jenkins of Chatham, Ontario, became the first Canadian to enter the Hall when he was inducted in 1991. During his illustrious career, Fergy was awarded the Cy Young in 1971, and won 20 games for six consecutive seasons en route to a career 284 wins. To top it all off, he threw over 3,000 strikeouts in his career.

4. Who was the first Toronto Blue Jay?

A. Before the Jays and the Seattle Mariners made their choices in the expansion lottery, the Jays, knowing they needed a veteran who could nurture and lead some of the youngsters, acquired veteran catcher Phil Roof from the Chicago White Sox on October 22, 1976. Unfortunately, Roof didn't prove to be the asset the Jays had hoped, and they dumped him faster than hot tar after he had played in only three games.

5. Pitcher Jack Graney was responsible for a number of firsts that will go down in the history of baseball. What were they?

A. Little-known pitcher Graney, a native of St. Thomas, Ontario, was the first player to wear a numbered jersey so the fans could readily recognize him. Secondly, when his active career ended he was the first player to start broadcasting games on radio for the Cleveland Indians. The third and possibly most impressive accomplishment is that he was the first major leaguer to pitch to Babe Ruth.

6. Did Pete Rose ever play baseball in Canada?

A. Charlie Hustle was one of the most intense players ever to play the sport of baseball. Canadians had the pleasure of calling him a hometown hero when he suited up for the Montreal Expos in 1984. Rose appeared in 95 games for the Expos and hit .259.

7. Who was "Le Grande Orange"?

A. Monsieur Orange was Rusty Staub, one of the most popular players ever to wear a Montreal Expos uniform. Staub was with the club for three full seasons, from 1969–1971, before moving on to New York, where he spent the rest of his career with the Mets until his retirement in the mid-1980s.

8. Where did Babe Ruth hit his first professional home run?

A. The legendary Bambino started his pro career as a pitcher for the Providence Grays. On September 15, 1914, at the old Island Stadium in Toronto, he belted out his first professional homer in a game against the Toronto Maple Leafs.

9. What event in Canadian sports history occurred on October 24, 1992?

A. That is the date when the Toronto Blue Jays became the first team from outside the United States to win the World Series. Who can forget that feeling of drama when the Atlanta Braves and the Jays tied and the game went into extra innings. It was in the top of the 11th inning that Blue Jay DH Dave Winfield doubled home two runs, and pitcher Mike Timlin held off a Braves rally to enable the Blue Jays to win their first of two consecutive world championships.

10. Who is the only Canadian to win the National League's Most Valuable Player award?

A. Maple Ridge, B.C. native Larry Walker has been absolutely outstanding throughout his career, winning batting championships, hitting almost 250 homers, and yes, being picked as the National League MVP in 1997. It looks like one of these days Ferguson Jenkins will have some Canadian company at the Baseball Hall of Fame.

11. Is it true that a Canadian invented the baseball glove?

A. It seems that a pretty good shortstop by the name of Art Irwin, who was playing for the Providence Grays, broke two of his fingers while catching the ball with his bare hand in the pre-glove era. Always a clever guy, he bought himself a large buckskin glove and after stuffing it with a little extra padding, the baseball mitt was born. Within a few years gloves were standard issue in America's game.

12. What Toronto Blue Jay third baseman also won the John Wooden Award as the U.S. College Basketball Player of the Year?

A. It was Danny Ainge who was chosen in the 1978 draft by the Jays. The Brigham Young University graduate was one of those two-sport athletes, and in addition to his abilities on the diamond, he was also one of the finest basketball talents in the country, hence the Wooden award. Ainge was chosen in the 1981 NBA draft by the Boston Celtics. The Blue Jays were so high on Ainge's talent that they paid him $300,000 to not switch sports. Unfortunately, the pay-off couldn't keep Ainge in Toronto, and after three seasons with the Jays he returned the $300,000 and headed to Boston to begin what turned out to be a very successful basketball career. Ainge would later play for the Sacramento Kings and the Phoenix Suns. After retiring he went onto a very successful coaching career in the NBA.

13. Did Canadian George "Moon" Gibson ever play on a World Series team?

A. The London, Ontario-born Gibson had a lengthy baseball career both as a major league player and manager. Born in 1880, the athletic Gibson played industrial league ball before becoming a catcher with Buffalo in the International League. By 1905 he was in the big leagues with Pittsburgh; in 1909 his team won the World Series, beating Detroit and their star Ty Cobb. In 1919, he turned to managing in the majors until his retirement in 1934. He played over 1,200 games in the major leagues and was known as one of the best defensive players of the era.

14. Who was the first Canadian pitcher to start in a World Series?

A. Reggie Cleveland of Swift Current, Saskatchewan, had this honour on October 16, 1975, when as a member of the Boston Red Sox he faced the Cincinnati Reds in Game 5 of the World Series. The Sox lost the game 6–2, and the Reds ended up winning the series 4 games to 3. Cleveland stayed in the big leagues for 13 seasons, retiring in 1981 after compiling a 105–106 record with a 4.02 ERA.

15. What do Canadians Helen Nicol, Olive Little, and Helen Callahan all have in common?

A. All three were players with the All-American Girls Professional Baseball League in the U.S. If you ever saw the movie "A League of Their Own" with Geena Davis, Tom Hanks, and Madonna, you know the history behind this very competitive women's baseball organization that operated from 1943 to 1954. What you may not know is that along with the three above mentioned ladies, there were 50 more from Canada who played in the league over the years, accounting for about 10% of all players in league history.

16. Was baseball first played in Canada?

A. Until recently many people believed it was. There have been published reports that a baseball game took place on June 4, 1838, in Beachville, Ontario, just outside of London, a year before Abner Doubleday supposedly invented the game in Cooperstown, New York. In July 2001, American sports historians discovered two newspaper articles from 1823 about a game of baseball played in Manhattan.

17. Has a professional baseball player ever gone to jail for assaulting an umpire in Canada?

A. It all started during the summer of 1907 when Tim Flood, a player with the Toronto Maple Leafs of the International League, was incensed over what he considered to be a bad call by umpire John Conway. Flood ran up and drop-kicked the surprised official in the chest, knocking him to the ground. A police inspector who witnessed the attack came out on the field and arrested Flood on the charge of assault. The judge was unsympathetic to the defence; because it had happened during a sporting event, Flood should be exempt from prosecution. The judge sentenced Flood to 15 days of hard labour. He was released after serving a week of the sentence, reportedly weighing about ten pounds less than when he went in.

18. Did the great Jackie Robinson ever play professional baseball in Canada?

A. It was in 1946 that Branch Rickey of the Brooklyn Dodgers had Robinson sign with the Triple-A Montreal Royals of the International League, a year before his debut as the first African-American player to break the colour barrier in the major leagues. The talented twenty-seven-year-old first baseman led the league in hitting with a .349 average to the delight of the Montreal fans who adored him. It's said that he always remembered how well he was treated here and had a soft spot in his heart for Montreal.

19. Is it true that a Canadian broke the colour barrier in baseball before Jackie Robinson?

A. Thirty years before Jackie Robinson broke baseball's colour barrier, a Canadian from New Westminster, British Columbia, attempted to do the same in a more round-about way. In 1916, Jimmy Claxton, an African-Canadian, caught on with the Oakland team of the Pacific Coast League. It seems that back then even in the minor leagues a colour barrier existed, but Claxton got around it by claiming to be a Native Indian. He was able to keep up the pretense for a good part of the 1916 season before he was found out. Another interesting offshoot of this situation: Claxton became the first black to ever have his picture presented on a baseball card.

20. Who was known as the "Terminator"?

A. Not too many baseball fans will ever forget Tom Henke, the six-foot-five right-hander from Kansas City, Missouri, who, as a member of the Toronto Blue Jays, was one of the most successful relief pitchers of his era. Henke joined the Jays in 1985 when he was acquired from the Texas Rangers. He stayed with the club until the 1992 season, in which he played an important role in the Jays' first World Series win. Henke jumped ship after the 1992 win, signed back on with the Texas Rangers, then ended his career in 1995 with the St. Louis Cardinals. He retired with a total of 311 saves, 217 of them for the Jays, and an ERA of 2.67.

21. In 1941, Ted Williams batted .406, and Joe DiMaggio hit safely in 56 consecutive games. What Canadian major leaguer outhit both stars that season?

A. Born in Fort William, Ontario, in 1915, Jeff Heath was a two-time all-star who had a career year in 1941 as a member of the Cleveland Indians. He was the first player in American League history to hit the triple-20 mark, which is 20 doubles, 20 triples, and 20 home runs in one season. He also had a total of 199 hits, which was more than Williams or DiMaggio hit that year. Another highlight for Heath was that at the All-Star game that season he got to share the American League outfield with Williams and DiMaggio.

22. How many World Series rings does Toronto Blue Jays' former team physician Dr. Ron Taylor possess?

A. Dr. Taylor has a grand total of four World Series rings in his possession, two as a result of the Blue Jays' back-to-back wins in 1992 and 1993, and two from his previous career as a major league relief pitcher. This Toronto-native had a ten-year career in the National League, pitching a total of 800 innings and posting a regular season ERA of 3.93. The amazing stat on Taylor's record is his perfect 0.00 average in post-season play with the 1964 St. Louis Cardinals and the 1969 New York Mets. The talented doctor and ballplayer is a member of both the Canadian Sports Hall of Fame and the Canadian Baseball Hall of Fame.

23. What was the Pearson Cup?

A. Named after our late Prime Minister and Nobel Prize winner Lester Pearson, this annual game was played between Canada's two major league teams, the Expos and the Blue Jays. The proceeds from these contests were put to good use, benefiting Canadian amateur baseball programs. The first game was played in Montreal on June 29, 1978, with the Expos edging the Jays 5–4. In all, eight games were played between 1978 and the final Pearson Cup in 1986 (no game was played in 1981 due to the players' strike). Each team won three cups, with two games ending in ties: the 1979 game was called a tie because the Expos had to catch a team flight, and the 1985 game was called after 11 innings because of time restraints.

24. What Canadian author has become renowned for his books and short stories on baseball?

A. Edmonton-born W.P. Kinsella has become one of the most respected authors on the sport of baseball, penning such classics as *Shoeless Joe* (made into the movie *Field of Dreams* with Kevin Costner), and the short story collection *The Thrill of the Grass*, along with many other novels and short stories celebrating baseball.

25. What Canadian-born major league relief pitcher set a record by recording 38 saves in a season?

A. Born in Toronto in 1943, John Hiller spent 15 years with the Detroit Tigers as one of the premier relievers in the game. His career year was 1973 when he compiled 38 saves — a major league record that would stand for a decade until broken by Kansas City's Don Quisenberry in 1983. What made Hiller's accomplishment all the more amazing was that only two seasons earlier he had suffered a serious heart attack many thought would end his career. But the tough Hiller brushed away adversity and bounced back to not only set that relief record, but to win the American League Comeback Player of the Year and Fireman of the Year awards in 1973. He stayed at the top of his game until his retirement in 1980.

John Hiller

26. What incredible coincidence occurred to the Toronto Blue Jays during a stretch of three games in June 1978?

A. The story begins with the Jays losing three consecutive games, one to the Detroit Tigers and a couple to the Texas Rangers. Now it's not the three-game losing streak that makes these games memorable, but the fact that all three losses came at the hands of Canadian pitchers. Against the Tigers, the Jays lost to Toronto's own John Hiller, and in the first two games in a series against the Texas Rangers, they lost to starting pitchers Reggie Cleveland of Swift Current, Saskatchewan, and Hall of Famer Ferguson Jenkins of Chatham, Ontario.

27. Where is the Canadian Baseball Hall of Fame located?

A. Just a couple of miles from Beachville, Ontario — where the first known Canadian game took place in 1838 — you can find the Hall in the small town of St. Mary's. The museum was formed in October 1983 with a mandate to preserve Canadian baseball heritage. To date, 48 people have been inducted into the Hall, including such greats as Ferguson Jenkins, George Selkirk, and Jack Graney. In the summer of 2001, the Hall opened its doors to former Montreal Expo Gary Carter and the Blue Jays' Dave McKay of Vancouver.

BASKETBALL

1. Did a Canadian invent the sport of basketball?

A. It was on December 21, 1891, in Springfield, Massachusetts, that Dr. James Naismith, a Y.M.C.A. instructor from Almonte, Ontario, invented basketball as a way for his charges to get some strenuous exercise. He originally used a soccer ball and two peach baskets perched at opposite ends of a gymnasium. Another interesting fact is that half of the ten players on that original Springfield basketball team were also Canadian.

2. Were the Toronto Raptors and the Vancouver Grizzlies Canada's first pro basketball teams?

A. No. In 1946, the Toronto Huskies came to life. They were part of the Basketball Association of America, a forerunner of the NBA. Unfortunately, we couldn't get the proper fan support for the team and the Huskies folded after just one season in the league. It would be half a century before pro basketball would return to the native home of its founder.

James Naismith

3. Has Canada ever won an Olympic medal in basketball?

A. It was only once during the infamous 1936 Olympics that Canada ever made it to the medal round. After winning their first five games they faced off against the heavily favoured American squad for the gold medal. The Americans won the game 19–8, and, in a touching moment, the gold medal was presented to the victors by Dr. James Naismith, the Canadian inventor of the game.

4. Who were the Edmonton Grads?

A. The Grads were probably the most successful team statistically in sports history. This ladies team dominated the sport

Percy Page with the Edmonton Grads

of basketball for a quarter of a century from the team's inception in 1915 to its disbandment in 1940. The Grads compiled an incredible record of 502 victories against only 22 defeats. And even though women's basketball wasn't yet an official event, the Grads competed in exhibition tournaments during the course of four Olympics, winning 27 consecutive games against the finest ladies' teams in the world. One of the Grads' biggest boosters was Canadian James Naismith, who was truly in awe of this talented group of athletes. Quite a fair bit of the team's success has to be attributed to their coach, John Percy Page. A legend himself, after the Grads disbanded he went on to a career as a politician in the Alberta Legislature and then served as the province's Lieutenant-Governor from 1959–1966.

5. Who was Noel MacDonald and what sport did she star in?

A. The Saskatchewan-born, Edmonton-raised, five-foot-ten beauty was one of the best basketball players ever developed in Canada. As a member of the infamous, all-woman Edmonton

Noel MacDonald

Grads, she led the team in scoring with an average of 13.8 points per game from her rookie year 1933 to her retirement from the Grads in 1939. A modest individual, she never enjoyed being singled out as a star player, but was a firm believer in the team-first philosophy that helped make the Grads one of the greatest teams in sports history. After her retirement, she coached at the high school level, and was an executive of the Canadian Amateur Basketball Association.

6. Who was the NBA's Rookie of the Year in 1995?

A. Damon Stoudamire was a five-foot-ten point guard out of the University of Arizona when he was chosen in the first round, seventh overall, by the expansion Toronto Raptors in the 1995 draft. He was the young superstar-hopeful the Raptors wanted to build the team around. He didn't disappoint them; the Mighty Mouse showed early that he belonged in the big leagues, averaging 19 points per game in that inaugural season with the Raptors, playing roughly 40 minutes per game. His star really shone when during the all-star break he was named the MVP in the league's all-rookie game. At season's end, Stoudamire's efforts were rewarded with the Rookie of the Year Award. Unfortunately, Stoudamire didn't seem happy in Toronto, so a couple of years later he was traded to his hometown Portland Trailblazers.

7. What was the Naismith Cup?

A. The Naismith Cup was played during the NBA pre-season for Canadian bragging rights between the now-defunct Vancouver Grizzlies and the Toronto Raptors. Named after the sport's Canadian inventor, the game was always played in a different, neutral city each year, allowing other Canadians a chance to witness a pro-basketball game live. Toronto dominated the series, taking four of the five games, starting with the inaugural game in 1995 in Winnipeg and ending with the 2000 game in Ottawa. The 1998 game was never played because of the NBA lockout that year.

8. What Canadian-based basketball star was named Rookie of the Year in 1998–99?

A. Selected fifth overall out of North Carolina by the Golden State Warriors, Vince Carter was immediately traded to Toronto for his college teammate Antawn Jamison. Carter took naturally to the pressures of NBA life, not only winning the rookie crown but also being the only rookie in the league to lead his team in scoring. Arguably the best slam dunker in the league, Carter has worked hard to also become one of the finest offensive players in the game. He led Toronto on their 2001 playoff drive where they lost in seven games to the Philadelphia 76ers in the conference semi-finals. A well-rounded, grounded, young man, Carter graduated in 2001 from the University of North Carolina with a degree in African-American studies.

9. Which Canadian-born professional basketball player's mother competed for Canada in the Olympic Games?

A. Born in Toronto, Rick Fox has had a solid career in the NBA since being drafted out of North Carolina in the first round of the 1991 draft. A member of the L.A. Lakers since the 1997–98 season, Rick isn't the only one in the family to have had a successful sports career. Five years before he was born, his mother, Toronto's own Dianne Gerace, was front and centre at the 1964 Tokyo Olympics, trying to win a gold medal in high-jump. Unfortunately, Gerace came up a little short, finishing in fifth spot with a 1.71-metre leap.

10. What long-time Canadian basketball team player is now head coach of our national squad?

A. One of the most solid players to play hoops for Canada, Niagara Falls' own Jay Triano has really done it all in the world of Canadian basketball. After a stellar career at Simon Fraser University, he was a member of the national team from 1978–88 — eight of those years as team captain. When his playing career was over, Triano took over as head coach at his alma mater, and in 1999 and 2000 coached the national team to a silver medal at the Tournament of the America's and a seventh-place finish at the Sydney Olympics. Most recently, Triano worked for the Vancouver Grizzlies, both as part of the team's commentating team and as a high-profile figure in their front office.

11. Was professional basketball played in Canada in the 1970s?

A. We did have some games played in the Toronto Maple Leaf Gardens in the mid-1970s, even though we ourselves didn't have a franchise at the time. The Buffalo Braves had joined the NBA in 1970, and within a few years had established themselves as an exciting, if inconsistent, team, featuring such young stars as Bob McAdoo and Ernie DeGregorio. The biggest problem the Braves seemed to have was consistently putting fans in their seats, and in the mid-70s tried to experiment playing a number of home games at the hockey shrine. The games sold quite well, and Maple Leafs and Gardens owner Harold Ballard at one point made overtures to the Braves and the NBA about possibly pur-chasing the team and moving it to Toronto. Unfortunately, the deal couldn't be finalized and in 1978 the Buffalo Braves became the San Diego Clippers, later moving to their present home in Los Angeles.

12. Who did the Vancouver Grizzlies draft first for their inaugural 1995 season?

A. The seven-foot tall, 290-pound centre Bryant "Big Country" Reeves was chosen in the first round, sixth overall, by the expansion Grizzlies. Born in 1973 in Fort Smith, Arkansas, this massive athlete was a standout in his collegiate at Oklahoma State. Even though Reeves never really panned out as the franchise player the Grizzlies had hoped for, he has developed into a pretty solid NBA player.

13. Where was the first ever NBA game played?

A. Even though it wasn't called the NBA yet, the Basketball Association of America was the direct forerunner to the NBA. The new pro league made it's first appearance when the New York Knickerbockers met the Toronto Huskies at Toronto's Maple Leaf Gardens on November 1, 1946. Ticket prices ranged all the way from 75 cents in the cheap seats to the astronomical price of $2.50 in the reds. By the way, the Knicks won the game by the score of 68–66. Fifty years later, on November 1, 1996, the NBA held a special golden anniversary, scheduling the New York Knicks to play the Raptors in Toronto.

14. Which Canadian city was granted their NBA franchise first, Vancouver or Toronto?

A. With the NBA going outside the U.S. for the first time in almost 50 years, it was Toronto who was the first to receive the franchise when on November 4, 1993, the NBA Board of Governors awarded the 28th league team to the city. On April 27, 1994, they announced that the NBA's 29th franchise would be awarded to the city of Vancouver. Both teams made their NBA debuts on November 3, 1995, with the Raptors coming out on top of the New Jersey Nets 94–79 and the Grizzlies pawing their way over the Portland Trailblazers 92–80.

BOXING

1. What sporting feat was accomplished by a man who later in his life won an Academy Award for Best Supporting Actor?

A. Victor McLagelen was an actor who could play a big, boozy, tough, big-hearted Irishman like no other. But he also knew how to throw a punch, and in Vancouver on March 10, 1909, climbed into the squared circle and challenged Jack Johnson for the heavyweight championship of the world. He in fact fought the champ to a "No Decision," which is kind of like a draw today. It was 26 years later that he won an Oscar for his role in The Informer. McLagelen also co-starred in such classics as Fort Apache and The Quiet Man with his friend John Wayne.

2. Who did Muhammed Ali fight in Edmonton in 1981?

A. The Greatest took on Edmonton Oiler tough-guy Dave Semenko in a charity exhibition and from some eyewitness accounts, Semenko didn't look out of place in the ring. Some may even say he looked better in the ring than on the rink.

3. Which Canadian amateur boxing champion, and hands-on favourite for gold, boycotted the 1936 Berlin Olympics in protest over Hitler's anti-semetic policies?

A. Sammy Luftspring decided that to compete in the Games would dishonour his Jewish heritage, and after a lot of soul searching decided to stay home and turn pro. He was having a lot of success until an eye injury forced him into an early retirement. Things turned out well for Sammy though, and he ended up having successful careers as an author, referee, and businessman.

4. Who was know as the "Boston Tar Baby"?

A. Sam Langford was one of the greatest fighters in the world never to get a world title shot. He was born in Weymouth, Nova Scotia, in 1880, but ran away from home at the age of 12. After beginning his pugilistic career, it was soon evident that Langford was something special. Unfortunately, no one wanted to put their title on the line against him and Langford was forced to fight unimportant fights for very little money. Tragically, he went blind after his career ended in the 1920s. He was helped by friends and lived in a nursing home until his death in 1956.

5. What was boxing super-promoter Bob Arum's first foray into the sweet science?

A. Arum, a lawyer by trade, who even worked as a Government Attorney for some of the Kennedy's Task Forces, dove into the world of boxing in a big way, helping promote the 1965 WBA heavyweight title fight between champion Ernie Terrel and Canadian George Chuvalo. The fight, which lost Arum and his partners a lot of money, nonetheless gave Arum his first look into the potential of the sport to generate huge profits. If you ever get a chance to see a tape of the fight, check out the terrible decision they gave to Terrel. Chuvalo clearly dominated most of the fight and should have been crowned champ.

6. What did Roberto Duran do in Canada on June 20, 1980?

A. He handed Sugar Ray Leonard the first loss of his professional career and won Leonard's WBC welterweight championship at Montreal's Olympic Stadium. The victory for Duran was to be short-lived, as five months later in New Orleans, Leonard defeated Duran in the infamous "no mas" bout where Duran unexpectedly quit in the fifth round.

7. What is former Olympic silver medalist and Canadian Heavyweight champion Willie DeWitt doing with himself since retiring from boxing?

A. This is one ex-fighter whose story has a happy ending. DeWitt, after winning the silver medal at the 1984 Games, turned pro and was going gangbusters until he faced a hungry Smokin' Bert Cooper and was stopped in two rounds. Not long after, Willie tragically lost his dad and brother in a helicopter accident, forcing him to rethink his priorities. After defeating Henry Tillman — the man who beat him for the Olympic gold medal — Willie retired a winner. DeWitt went to law school after his career ended, and he and his family live in Alberta where he's part of a thriving law practice.

8. Vince McMahon of the WWF tested the waters once and promoted a world title fight with a definite Canadian connection. What was the fight?

A. On November 7, 1988, McMahon promoted the WBC super middleweight bout between Canadian Donny Lalonde of Winnipeg and champion Sugar Ray Leonard. Despite being knocked down a couple of times in the fight, Leonard came back to TKO Lalonde in ninth round. As it turned out, this was McMahon's last endeavour as a boxing promoter.

9. Who did Lennox Lewis defeat to win his gold medal at the 1988 Seoul Olympics?

A. Lewis dominated the heavyweight division of the Games, needing only 10 minutes and 16 seconds to get rid of his three opponents. For the gold medal match he stopped another future world champion, Riddick Bowe, at 43 seconds into the second round. As much as their professional bout was highly anticipated, it unfortunately never got off the ground due to boxing politics.

10. Who was the only Canadian-born heavyweight champion of the world?

A. Even though Trevor Berbick and Lennox Lewis were Canadian citizens, the only world champion who was actually born in Canada was Tommy Burns (born Noah Brusso), in Hanover, Ontario, in 1881. He won the world title by pummeling Marvin Hart in February 1906, and proved himself a fighting champion by defending his title ten times in less than three years. He lost the crown on Boxing Day 1908 to Jack Johnson.

12. Did Nova Scotia's Clyde Gray ever fight for the world welterweight title?

A. Clyde actually had two cracks at the gold with the first being on September 22, 1973, at Toronto's Maple Leaf Gardens when he lost a unanimous decision to the great Jose Napoles. He got a second kick at the can on June 28, 1975, when he lost another decision to Angel Espada. The long-time Canadian and Commonwealth champ was managed by well-known Canadian sports promoter and chicken magnate Irving Ungerman.

13. Did an American citizen ever win a gold medal for Canada in the sport of boxing?

A. As strange as it seems it really did happen at the 1920 Antwerp Olympics. Bert Schnieder of Montreal won a gold medal for us in the sport of boxing. The talented welterweight was born in Cleveland, Ohio, and had come to Canada as a very young boy. While the Schnieders were still all technically Americans, the twenty-three-year-old Bert was given permission to fight for the only country he knew in his life.

14. Did a professional boxer ever get KO'd by a referee in Canada?

A. In 1971, at the swank Royal York Hotel in Toronto, Canada's own Clyde Gray was facing Umberto Trottman. Trottman gave the referee — former 1940s welterweight contender Sammy Luftspring — a tough time from the start, refusing to follow the ref's orders. Then, suddenly, Trottman threw a shot at the ref, who, though in his late 50s, proved to be more than a match for Trottman, and countered with a crisp combination that knocked out the surprised fighter. Gray was awarded the victory by disqualification.

15. Who did Mathew Hilton defeat to become the IBF junior middleweight champion?

A. The fighting Hiltons of Montreal are the most successful and controversial boxing family in Canada. Mathew won his title in his hometown by pounding out a decision over American Buster Drayton in 1987. He held the title a little over a year, losing it in Las Vegas in November 1988 to Robert Hines. Hilton has since retired from boxing due to a severe eye injury.

16. Who was the first black man to win a boxing world championship?

A. George "Little Chocolate" Dixon was born in Halifax in 1870. Turning pro at the age of 16, he was racking up an amazing record when he travelled to England in 1890 and proceeded to knock out Nunc Wallace in the 18th round, winning the world bantamweight championship. He then moved up in weight class, and the next year won the featherweight title from Abe Attell with a fifth round KO. He finally lost his title for good when he was knocked out by Terry McGovern in January 1900. This terrific pugilist made the entire country proud of this small, slight man with the heart of a heavyweight.

17. How many times did George Chuvalo fight for the world heavyweight championship?

A. Even though the long-time Canadian champ fought Muhammed Ali twice — in 1966 and 1972 — only the first fight was for the title. In the second fight, Ali was on the comeback trail and didn't have the title at the time. The first fight in Toronto in March 1966 was actually the second title shot Chuvalo earned — the first being in 1965 when he lost an extremely controversial decision to WBA champion Ernie Terrel of the U.S.

George Chuvalo

18. Can you name the Montreal-based fighter who won the WBC super middleweight championship in the year 2000?

A. Davey Hilton Jr. comes from a very successful but controversial family, and fights out of Montreal. Davey was poised and ready for a world title shot back in the 80s before he was sidelined with a serious knee injury sustained in a motorcycle accident. His career saw many setbacks before it really got going again in the late 90s when he beat the rising French Canadian star Stephan Ouelett in two out of three bouts. Those wins propelled Hilton into a world title shot, and in the fall of 2000 he defeated Dingaan Thobela of Africa for the super middleweight title. Hilton was later stripped of his title due to a sexual assault conviction that saw him sentenced to a lengthy jail term.

19. Who was Ovila Chapdelaine and what sport was this Canadian a world champion in?

A. You can look in all the record books you want and you won't find this St. Francis, Quebec native listed in any of them. That's because when the light heavyweight boxer turned pro his manager insisted he change his name to Jack Delaney. Everyone knew when he turned pro in 1919 that there was something special about this two-fisted ring stylist. His career peaked when on July 16, 1926, in front of 45,000 fans in Brooklyn's Ebbett's Field, he decisioned American Paul Berlenbach for his world title. Delaney, who held the title for over a year, retired from the sport in 1932, and is now a member of the Canadian Sports Hall of Fame.

20. Who was known as the "Fighting Fisherman"?

A. Yvon Durelle was a fighter by nature so it was only natural for the Baie Ste. Anne, New Brunswick native to fight for a living in the boxing world. He showed excellent promise early in his career, and shortly after turning pro won first the Canadian middleweight and then the light heavyweight championship. Yvon rose in the world rankings and in 1958 he got his big break facing off against world champion Archie Moore. Yvon shocked the world by dropping Moore several times in the early rounds, but then tired and was stopped in the eleventh round. To this day it is one of the most discussed fights in Canadian history. Durelle was later given a rematch, but the bout was anti-climatic with Yvon being stopped in the early rounds. Yvon retired from the sweet science in the early 60s and spent his remaining days as a fisherman and a bar owner.

21. Which Canadian boxer won the world welterweight title twice back in the 1930s?

A. Born in Ireland but raised in Vancouver since the age of three, Jimmy McLarnin became one of the most exciting fighters of his era. After turning pro in the States, his career skyrocketed, and within a few years he was headlining cards at Madison Square Garden. He beat some terrific fighters by the likes of Sammy Mandell, Bill Petrolle, and Benny Leonard. All of these wins led him to his world title shot against Young Corbett III, who the Canadian demolished in just one round. A year later he lost his title to the great Barney Ross by decision, only to regain it some months later. The rubber match was held at the New York Polo Grounds in May 1935, and McLarnin lost to Ross by decision, in what some sportswriters called a savage display of pugilism. McLarnin retired soon after the fight and prospered as a businessman. He was chosen in 1950 as Canadian Boxer of the Half-Century.

Jimmy McLarnin

22. Did former heavyweight champion Floyd Patterson ever defend his title in Canada?

A. Yes, he did, and it turned out to be the very last defence of his belt before being demolished the next year by Sonny Liston. On December 4, 1961, Patterson faced off against Boston's Tom McNeely at Toronto's Maple Leaf Gardens and dominated the challenger, knocking him in the fourth round. Interestingly, McNeely is the father of sacrificial Peter McNeely, who was Mike Tyson's first opponent after the former heavyweight champ's release from his three-year prison term.

23. Who did Trevor Berbick defeat on December 11, 1981?

A. Trevor Berbick, originally from Jamaica but now living in Halifax, Nova Scotia, climbed into the ring that evening in the Bahamas to meet a forty-year-old overweight shell of what once was probably the greatest heavyweight champion of all time, Muhammed Ali. Ali lost the fight to the lumbering Berbick, and finally accepted the inevitable and retired for good. Berbick went on to win the WBC version of the title in 1985, which he lost to a young Mike Tyson.

24. Which boxing junior middleweight won a silver medal for Canada at the 1984 Los Angeles Olympics?

A. Toronto-born and raised Shawn O'Sullivan took this country by storm after winning the world amateur championships in 1981. Going into the Olympics, he was an odds on favourite for the gold medal, but was upset by American Frank Tate in the final match. After turning pro, he caught the eye of Sugar Ray Leonard, who became part of his advisory and management team. Unfortunately, his style was better suited to the amateurs, and after some dramatic losses the Olympic hero decided to retire. Shawn made two comeback attempts in the early and mid-1990s, but never regained the form of his younger years.

25. What junior welterweight won a silver medal in boxing at the 1992 Barcelona Olympics?

A. Marc Leduc has been an inspirational figure to many Canadians. This young man has faced many adversities in his life: he went from a street kid to doing a stretch at Kingston Penitentiary to making the 1992 Canadian Olympic boxing team. Leduc was not considered to be one of the favourites at Barcelona, but showed great skills and grit to make it to the gold medal round where he lost to Cuba's Hector Vincent. Leduc turned pro after the Games, having limited success. He briefly held the Canadian junior welterweight title, but by the mid-90s decided to retire from the sport to pursue other interests.

26. What Canadian heavyweight boxer defeated both Max Schmeling and Primo Carnera?

A. In the course of his long career, Toronto heavyweight Larry Gaines KO'd the soon-to-be world champion Max Schmeling in 1925, outpointed the Italian giant Primo Carnera in 1932, and lost a close decision to number-one ranked heavyweight Tommy Farr in 1939. Gaines continued his successful career on May 18, 1934, when he won the British Empire heavyweight championship by defeating George Cook in London. This championship had been created especially for Gaines by his promoters: Gaines had been unable to get a British title shot because of a colour barrier that existed in England at the time.

27. What Canadian fighter defeated former heavyweight champ Floyd Patterson's son for the IBF junior light-weight championship?

A. It was Montreal-born Arturo Gatti who walked into the ring a contender and left a champion when he decisioned American Tracey Harris Patterson for his crown. Fighting out of New Jersey, Gatti was a breath of fresh air in the sport and a throw back to the old days of boxing — an exciting slugger who gave no quarter. Immensely popular with fans, Gatti defended his title three times before giving it up due to difficulties making the 130-pound weight limit. Gatti moved up to the heavier weight divisions, but, against more powerful competition, lost some crucial fights to top talents like Ivan Robinson and Angel Manfredy. Nevertheless, the always dangerous Gatti remained a top contender. On March 24, 2001, in the biggest and probably most lucrative bout of his career, Arturo faced Oscar de la Hoya, and was stopped in the fifth round.

28. What native Hamiltonian held a boxing world championship?

A. It was featherweight champion Jackie Callura. Jackie was born into a big but poor Italian family in Hamilton's north end. By the age of nine, he was taking part in what were called "Friday night smokers," illegal fights held in local gyms and bar rooms. This tough little kid started to build up quite a following, which led him to the Olympics at the young age of 15. The inexperienced Callura ended up out of the medals. Turning pro in 1936, he started making a name for himself as a tough brawler who could take as much as he could give out. The highlight of his career came in January 1943 when he decisioned Jackie Wilson in Providence, Rhode Island, for the NBA world championship. He lost the title only seven months later to American Phil Terranova when he was knocked out in the eighth round. After being stopped a few months later in the rematch, Callura was never a serious contender again.

29. What Canadian boxer made his pro debut by knocking out four fighters in one night?

A. On April 23, 1956, Canadian teenage sensation George Chuvalo won the Jack Dempsey tournament held in Toronto at Maple Leaf Gardens. In the round robin tourney, Chuvalo KO'd three fighters in the first round before dispatching American Gordie Baldwin to the showers in the second to win this highly regarded tourney. In total time, Chuvalo spent an extraordinary 12 minutes and 36 seconds defeating the four boxers.

30. What unusual event did George Foreman take part in Canada on April 26, 1975?

A. About six months after his loss to Muhammed Ali in Zaire, Foreman's promoters were looking for something that would get the ex-champ back on track and give the public a new angle to swallow. It was on April 26, 1975, at Maple Leaf Gardens that Foreman faced the challenge of having to defeat five opponents in one evening. Hardly top opponents, Charlie Polite, Boone Kinkman, Terry Daniels, Jerry Judge, and Alonzo Johnson were all dispatched of in a collective 12 rounds.

31. What former professional American boxer and subject of a popular movie now makes his home in Canada?

A. Born in Paterson, New Jersey, Rubin "Hurricane" Carter was a solid middleweight contender in the 1960s who lost a world title match in 1966 to Joey Giardello. In 1967, he was sentenced to life imprisonment for a triple murder and spent the next 20 years trying to prove his innocence. In the early 1980s, he was helped in his quest by a group of Canadians who learned of his situation by reading his book *The Sixteenth Round*. After several years of hard work, Carter was freed on November 7, 1985, when the judge in the case ruled that his conviction was based on racial prejudice and not the facts of the case. Carter moved to the Toronto area with the group of Canadian friends who did so much to help him get his freedom. Carter's life was turned into the Hollywood film *The Hurricane* starring Denzel Washington.

32. What legendary Canadian athlete has appeared in such movies as *The Fly*, *Prom Night III*, and *The Return of Elliot Ness*?

A. It's not hard to recognize long-time Canadian heavyweight champ and top world class contender George Chuvalo, even when it's on the big screen having his forearm torn off by Jeff Goldblum in *The Fly*.

FIGURE
SKATING

I. Did Toller Cranston ever win a gold medal in the Olympic Games?

A. No, he didn't make it all the way to gold, but the Hamilton, Ontario native did come in third to win a bronze medal at the 1976 Innsbruck Games. Many people felt that he got a raw deal from the judges who didn't seem to appreciate the Canadian's artistic genius.

2. Who was the first Canadian figure skater to win the Big Four — the Canadian, European, World, and Olympic titles — all in one year?

A. Barbara Ann Scott achieved this impressive first in 1948. Her skating style featured moves and jumps that influenced the sport for years to come; her charm and class have made all Canadians proud of this skating sweetheart. Over the years she has proven herself to be a superb ambassador of the sport for Canada.

3. How many times did Barbara Underhill and Paul Martini win the pairs' world championships?

A. Arguably one of the greatest pairs to ever compete in the skating world, they were world champions five times in the late 80s and early 90s. Their on-ice interpretation of "When a Man Loves a Woman" is generally regarded as one of the hottest routines in the history of the sport.

4. Don McPherson of Stratford, Ontario, had two incredible achievements in the world of figure skating in 1963. What were they?

A. First of all, young Don was the first skater to win the Canadian, North American, and world championships in one year. Secondly, he was the youngest male (18) to win the world championship. However, he never got the opportunity to complete the Big Four; as much as he wanted to compete in the 1964 Olympics, his financial conditions warranted him signing with "Holiday on Ice" and turning pro.

5. Has Canada ever won a gold medal in men's figure skating?

A. Even though Canadians have come close over the years, and have won their share of silver and bronze, the big prize has eluded us. Both Elvis Stojko and Brian Orser have won world championships but came up a little short at the Olympics. Luckily for us, our ladies and pairs have had a more luck in getting to the gold medal podium.

6. What former Canadian politician won a world championship in figure skating?

A. Otto Jelinik and his sister Maria were born in Czechoslovakia and immigrated to Canada when they were young. Their family settled in Oakville, Ontario, and it was there that they both showed their talent in pairs skating. After winning the Canadian junior championships they came in second in the world championships in 1960 to fellow Canadians Barbara Wagner and Robert Paul. After a fourth place finish at the 1960 Olympics, the team was ready to blossom, and two years later, at the 1962 world championships in their birth country of Czechoslovakia, Maria and Otto fulfilled their dream of winning the world championship. After turning pro with the Ice Capades they left the sport. Maria entered the travel business and Otto turned to federal politics, where he served a term as the Canadian Minister of Sports.

7. Which Canadian figure skater won the 1973 ladies' world championship?

A. Karen Magnussen learned to skate at almost the same time she learned to walk, and appeared in roles at winter carnivals at the age of 6. At the age of 14, she won over the crowd when she took fourth place in the Canadian championships. By 1968, she was the Canadian champ, and in 1969 was a favourite for a medal, placing in the worlds when a doctor discovered stress fractures in both of her legs. Fighting back from the injuries, she won the Canadian title for the next three years and placed well in the international meets. In 1973, everything came together for her when she won the world championships being held that year in Czechoslovakia. After the worlds, she turned pro and signed on with the Ice Capades. A few years later, Karen left the ice show and began to coach youngsters in Vancouver, where she also tested her entrepreneurial spirit by opening a successful restaurant.

8. Can you name Canada's first champion figure skater?

A. Figure skating in the late 1800s was very different from the sport we know today. The competition was basically based on an individual's ability to trace and retrace set figures on the ice.

Louis Rubenstein of Montreal won the Canadian championship in 1883 and held it for a full seven years. Along the way he won the U.S. championships back-to-back in 1888 and 1889 and received an invitation to compete at an informal "world championship" in St. Petersburg, Russia. What Mr. Rubenstein found in Russia was rampant anti-semitism, and he even had his passport seized and was ordered out of the country. It took intervention by the British Ambassador to straighten out this horrific treatment of Rubenstein. Despite the stressful conditions, Rubenstein proved to be the class of the competition, and left Russia with the championship in hand. After his skating retirement Rubenstein spent years promoting athletics, was named president of the Young Men's Hebrew Association in Montreal, and for years served the public as an alderman in Montreal.

9. Which female figure skater won a memorable silver medal for Canada at the 1988 Calgary Olympics?

A. Elizabeth Manley, a petite dynamo in a white cowboy hat, dazzled us all with her energetic performance on the ice, taking the silver medal in a near flawless performance. This Gloucester, Ontario-born competitor finished second in dramatic fashion, beating out American Debbie Thomas and finishing just behind East German Katerina Witt. After the Games, Liz decided to turn pro and signed on to perform with the Ice Capades. To this day Elizabeth appears in shows and competitions on the proskating circuit.

Kurt Browning

10. Which one of these figure skaters has won the most Canadian men's singles titles?

a. Kurt Browning
b. Elvis Stojko
c. Brian Orser

A. Born in Belleville, Ontario, Brian Orser won eight national championships from 1981–88, edging out Elvis Stojko's six national titles and Kurt Browning's four. On the world stage, these three competitors have combined to win 11 world titles over a twenty-year period.

11. What sports broadcasting pioneer was responsible for helping bring figure skating to the forefront, and was an announcer on the telecast of the 1972 Canada-Russia hockey series?

A. Battleford, Saskatchewan's Johnny Esaw is widely respected not only for his work in front of the camera, but also behind the scenes in helping promote Canadian sports and athletes. His work with the CTV network on the 1972 Canada-Russia hockey series as both an announcer and producer solidified his place in Canadian sports and broadcasting history. Esaw has always been given credit as one of the driving forces that elevated the sport of figure skating to its mainstream popularity through the powers of enhanced television coverage.

12. What did Petra Burka accomplish in Canadian sports history?

A. After Barbara Ann Scott's dominance of women's skating in the late 40s, Canadians went through a drought of almost 20

years. But in 1965, a pretty eighteen year old by the name of Petra Burka burst upon the scene to not only win the Canadian and North American championships, but also the most prestigious title of all, the world championship. Coached by her mother Ellen, this talented skater, who came to Canada from Holland at the age of 4, won all three championships in the space of one month — a feat that propelled

Petra Burka

her to sports stardom. After the world championships the next year in Switzerland, where she placed a respectable third, Petra then decided to join a professional ice show. This talented Canadian was inducted into the Canadian Sports Hall of Fame in 1965, and in 1996 was joined in that esteemed organization by her mother, who had achieved lasting success as the coach of such Canadian skating stars as Toller Cranston and Elvis Stojko.

13. What is the death spiral and what important connection does it have to Canada?

A. You've seen and marveled at this dangerous-looking move popular in pairs skating. The male lowers his partner to almost ice level, holds her hand, and swings her in a circular motion while she, lying almost flat, glides in the circular motion with her head just a couple of inches above ice level. This move was developed by Canadian pairs stars Suzanne Morrow and Wally Distelmeyer. They made Canadian sports history in 1948 not only with the debut of this innovative move, but by being the first Canadians to win medals in both the world championships and the Olympics. Each were also accomplished singles skaters, with Distelmeyer winning the Canadian title in 1948, and Miss Morrow winning Canadian championships in 1949, 1950, and 1951.

14. What former Canadian figure skating great has became a successful artist?

A. 1976 Olympic bronze medallist and six-time Canadian champion Toller Cranston in widely know as one of the most prominent figure skaters of his time. A native of Hamilton, Ontario, Cranston has had quite a career outside of competitive skating as a television commentator, author, and a painter whose works have been exhibited in galleries around the world.

15. Which Canadian skating pair won Olympic Gold in 1960, ending 36 years of European dominance?

A. Barbara Wagner and Robert Paul, both of Toronto, were singles skaters who shared the same coach — Sheldon Galbraith. It was Galbraith who first pictured them as a team, and after some convincing a partnership was born. Success came almost immediately to the young couple. In a span of two weeks in February 1957, they won the Canadian championships in Winnipeg, the North American title in New York, and the world championships in Colorado. They repeated their triple-crown success in 1958, 1959, and 1960. After four years of dominance, the Canadian pair went into the 1960 Squaw Valley Olympics as heavy favourites, and the Canadians didn't disappoint taking home the gold in what turned out to be their final competition. After the Olympics Wagner and Paul joined the Ice Capades show where they were popular headliners until their retirement a few years later.

FOOTBALL

1. What was the first American team to join the Canadian Football League?

A. The 1992 Sacramento Gold Miners were the first U.S. team to be a part of what turned out to be an unsuccessful expansion strategy by the league. What they hoped to accomplish was to sell our game to the Americans and try to financially solidify the league with the sponsorship money they thought would naturally follow. Alas, the dream failed, and three-down football is now completely Canadian again, the way many of us feel it should remain.

2. What does the CFL do every season that goes against the expressed wishes of the man who donated its championship trophy?

A. Since the CFL was officially formed in 1958, the Grey Cup has been in the hands of professional football teams. The funny thing is that when former Governor General Lord Grey donated the award, his wishes were that it would always remain played under amateur conditions.

3. Have NFL/AFL and CFL teams ever played each other?

A. Actually, NFL and CFL teams met several times in exhibitions and our boys did a pretty good job staying competitive with the Americans. The most recent game was in 1961, in Hamilton, when the Ti-Cats beat the AFL Buffalo Bills 38–21. After that, the American bigwigs refused to let their teams play us without league approval, and for reasons unknown, those exhibitions came to an end.

4. What year was the CFL founded?

A. Football in Canada has an incredibly rich history that goes back over a century, and leagues featuring top-notch talent have been around all that time. But while the Grey Cup has been contested since 1909, the league for which it has become a symbol didn't come into being until 1958.

5. Why was the 1962 Grey Cup played over the period of two days?

A. That year's Cup was played at Toronto's Exhibition Stadium on December 1 between the Hamilton Tiger-Cats and the Winnipeg Blue Bombers. During the second half, a heavy fog rolled off Lake Ontario and visibility was next to nothing. With about five minutes left in the game and the officials unable to see anything that was happening on the field, the game was halted, and it was ruled that the time left would have to be made up the next day. And so, on December 2, the game was finished, the

Bombers won 28–27, and the Fog Bowl was written into Canadian sports history.

6. How many Grey Cups did Doug Flutie win during his stay in the CFL?

A. Without a doubt Flutie was probably the single most exciting football player to play in Canada. After signing on with the B.C. Lions in 1990, his football heroics became historic. Flutie broke almost all records available to him en route to winning three Grey Cups during his Canadian career. The first championship came in 1992 with the Calgary Stampeders, and was followed by two consecutive crowns with the Argos in 1996 and 1997.

7. What famous CFL player was known as "The Rifle"?

A. Sam Etcheverry was one of the most dominant quarterbacks of the 1950s, passing for over 25,000 yards and setting numerous records — a few of which remain today. This proud Montreal Alouette was awarded the Schenley Award for Most Valuable Player in 1954, and twice won the Jeff Russell Award for Outstanding Player in the Eastern Division over a nine-year career.

8. What Canadian city has won the most Grey Cups?

A. It looks like Toronto all the way with a total of 21 wins. The Argos have won 14 of those, with the University of Toronto, the Balmy Beaches Club, and the R.C.A.F. Hurricanes making up the rest.

9. Which American team was the first to challenge for the Grey Cup?

A. In 1994, for the first time in history, an American team, the Baltimore Stallions, played for the Grey Cup when they faced the B.C. Lions. The Americans came up short, losing the game 26–23, and the Cup stayed in Canada for another year. Unfortunately, the American expansion failed, and within a couple of years our CFL was again a strictly Canadian game.

10. Did a fan ever get personally involved in a Grey Cup game?

A. It was in Toronto in 1957 when some moron ran out and tripped up Hamilton Ti-Cat Ray Bawel as he was running the ball in for a touchdown against the Winnipeg Blue Bombers. Hamilton ended up scoring later in the series and won the Cup 32–7. The offending tripper tried to make up for the incident by sending Bawel a gold watch. Considering the event and the circumstances, I hope it was a Rolex.

11. Which CFL team has lost the most Grey Cup games?

A. Well it's a tie, actually, between the Winnipeg Blue Bombers and the Hamilton Ti-Cats — each with 14 losses. On the other side of the coin, we should mention that up to the 2000 season, Hamilton has won 15 and Winnipeg 11 Cups, respectively.

12. Which coach has won the most games in the CFL?

A. On October 18, 1997, while coaching the Toronto Argonauts, Don Mathews passed Frank Clair for his 148th win in the CFL. Since breaking into the league as a coach in 1983, Mathews has won three Grey Cups, including the first one by a non-Canadian team, the 1995 Baltimore Stallions.

13. Does Doug Flutie have a brother who plays in the CFL?

A. It's got to be tough to play in Doug Flutie's shadow, but his kid brother Darren has done a pretty good job making it on his own exceptional abilities. After graduating from both his and his brothers alma mater, Boston College, Darren caught on with the San Diego Chargers and the Phoenix Cardinals before coming north in 1991. The fleet-footed receiver has been on two Grey Cup winners (up to the 2000 season) and has been a multi-year choice for the CFL all-star team.

14. What happened for the very first, and probably last, time in Regina on November 19, 1995?

A. A U.S.-based team, the Baltimore Stallions, won the Grey Cup by defeating the Calgary Stampeders 37–20. Baltimore was one of the American teams who joined the league in the mid-90s in a disastrous attempt to expand the CFL south of the border. By the next season, the Stallions had relocated north of the border and became the Montreal Alouettes.

15. What former CFL Hall of Fame quarterback became a school teacher after his retirement?

A. Russ Jackson, big number 12 of the Ottawa Rough Riders, was definitely one of the greatest players ever to play in the CFL. For over 40 years every great quarterback has been measured against this seven-time Schenley Winner (three as outstanding player, four as most outstanding Canadian). A perennial all-star, Jackson won Grey Cups in 1960, 1968, and 1969. Retiring at what

Russ Jackson

some say was his prime, Jackson became a school teacher and principal, but continued to stay close to the game, working as a commentator for the CFL.

16. Who were the "Gold Dust Twins"?

A. The Gold Dust Twins were one of the most talented tandems to ever play Canadian football. Joe Krol was the quarterback and Royal Copeland was his sure-handed receiver. Together they were pivotal in the Argos' three consecutive Grey Cup wins in 1945, 1946, and 1947.

Joe Krol was one of the absolute greats of the post-war league, leading the Argos to five total Grey Cup wins. He received the Lou Marsh Award in 1946 and the Canadian Press Athlete of the Year honour in 1947.

Royal Copeland, born in North Bay, Ontario, and spent a total of ten years with the Boatmen. He was probably the dominant receiver in his days before retiring and moving to California.

17. Which player has scored the most career touchdowns in CFL history?

A. In 13 seasons between 1963 and 1975, George Reed ran the ball into the end zone a league-record 137 times for the Saskatchewan Roughriders. Along with the touchdown record, he ran for an impressive 16,116 yards and had 11 seasons of rushing for more than 1,000 yards. Yet for all these accomplishments, Reed only won one Grey Cup, when his Roughriders defeated Ottawa 29–14 in 1966.

George Reed

18. What high-ranking politician led his team to a Grey Cup victory?

A. Quarterback Don Getty led his Edmonton Eskimos to a 50–27 upset win over the favourite Montreal Alouettes in the 1957 Grey Cup classic. Getty, who hails from Westmount, Quebec, scored two touchdowns while helping Jackie Parker with his three majors. It seems that Mr. Getty didn't do too badly after retiring from the game, serving as premier of Alberta from 1985–92.

19. Who won the very first Grey Cup game?

A. On Saturday, December 4, 1909, at Rosedale Field in Toronto, the University of Toronto defeated crosstown rivals Toronto Parkdale 26–6 in the first Grey Cup championship game. The scoring hero was Hugh Gall, who scored a touchdown and eight singles to lead his team to victory. Interestingly, the 4th Earl of Grey was not in attendance on this day — and in fact never saw a game contested for the trophy that bears his name.

20. Which CFL player holds the distinction of being chosen the most times as the league's most outstanding player?

A. That honour goes to Doug Flutie. The New England-born former Heisman Trophy winner shattered many a league record during his stay in the CFL, and won three Grey Cups. Along the way Flutie was chosen as the CFL's most outstanding player a total of six times, including four times in a row from 1991–94. His six wins eclipse the former record of three wins achieved by football greats Jackie Parker and Russ Jackson.

21. What two CFL teams played an exhibition game in New York City on December 11, 1909?

A. At the invitation of one of the Big Apple's most influential newspapers, the Hamilton Tigers and the Ottawa Rough Riders played an exhibition game at Van Cortland park in New York. It seems that some reporters witnessed one of our games and thought it would go over well in the U.S. The newspaper must have done a heck of a job publicizing the game, because over 15,000 people showed up to watch the Tigers beat the Rough Riders 11–6.

22. When did the first modern CFL game take place, and which teams took part in that game?

A. The CFL as we know it, featuring strictly professional teams and players, was formed on January 19, 1958. It opened its season on August 14 of that year in Winnipeg when the hometown Bombers defeated the Edmonton Eskimos 29–21 before 18,000 fans. Winnipeg was definitely the team of the year when on November 29, 1958, at Empire Stadium in Vancouver, the Blue Bombers defeated the Hamilton Tiger-Cats 35–28 in the first professionals-only Grey Cup Game.

23. Why did the Grey Cup game of 1912 almost get postponed?

A. The date was Saturday, November 30, and the Grey Cup was scheduled to be contested at the beautiful Hamilton Cricket Grounds. The hometown Hamilton Alerts were to play host to the heavily favoured Toronto Argonauts in the fourth edition of the battle for Lord Grey's cup. Everything was going as planned with a boisterous sold-out crowd in place, officials ready to administer to their duties, and a field full of players ready to do battle. Well it seems that the only thing forgotten in the preparations for this match was no one remembered to bring a football. Embarrassed officials went on a panicked search for a game pigskin with no luck until a stadium employee came across a locked storage room and, when a key couldn't be found, kicked down the door to reveal a lone football. The panic must have really helped the hometown Alerts, as they upset the favourite Argos 11–4.

24. Which late Canadian Supreme Court Justice played on the CFL?

A.John Sopinka could best be described as a man of many diverse talents. This Broderick, Saskatchewan-born, Hamilton-raised young man was quite a musical prodigy, and at the age of 15 made his debut as a violinist for the Hamilton Philharmonic.

An honour student and a natural athlete, Sopinka worked his way through law school as a pretty fair defensive halfback for first the Toronto Argos and later the Montreal Alouettes. He dropped football in 1958 to concentrate on his studies and soon afterwards passed his bar exam. A high-profile defence attorney, John was chosen to sit on the Supreme Court in 1988.

25. What former CFL star and professional wrestler was nick-named "King Kong"?

A.Angelo Mosca, a 6'4", 300-pound plus behemoth from New England came to Canada in 1958 after graduating from Notre Dame to try his hand at our brand of professional football. He played a total of 15 seasons in the CFL, most of them for the Hamilton Ti-Cats. Mosca was a member of five Grey Cup-winning teams, and won multiple individual honours during his football career. In the late 1960s, he started to wrestle part-time, and after retiring from football he took to the ring full-time, making quite a name for himself. For a while big Ange even promoted for the NWA putting together some big shows in Hamilton's Copps Coliseum. He still resides in the Hamilton area and devotes a lot of his time to charity work.

26. Did the World Football League have a team in Canada?

A. In 1974, John F. Bassett, son of the owner of the CFL's Toronto Argonauts, tried to forge his way into the world of pro football when the upstart World Football League granted him a franchise that was to be known as the Toronto Northmen. Bassett hired Leo Cahill to serve as coach and general manager of the new team, and together they went as far as stealing away three NFL stars from the Miami Dolphins — Larry Csonka, Paul Warfield, and Jim Kiick — and introducing them to Canadian audiences. But the government, especially Health Minister Marc Lalonde, was concerned that northward expansion by the WFL would have a negative impact on the homegrown CFL, and introduced Bill C-22 into Parliament. But the bill was never put to a vote in the House of Commons; the Northmen ownership, recognizing the government's resolve, moved the team lock, stock, and barrel to Memphis before a game was ever played on Canadian soil.

27. What Canadian actor was part owner of a CFL club?

A. The lovable, comedic actor John Candy joined his pal Wayne Gretzky and entrepreneur Bruce McNall in purchasing the Toronto Argonauts from Harry Ornest in 1991. From the very beginning they spent money to bring in marquee players, the most notable being Rocket Ishmail, the Notre Dame star they lured to the CFL with a cool $14-million contract. Their free-spending paid off quickly with the Argos winning the 1991 Grey Cup, but by the next season the team's fortunes had reversed. By 1994 McNall's financial empire was crumbling around him and the team was sold. But Gretzky had gotten his first taste of team ownership, and the role seemed to suit him — he has gone on to become a partner in the Phoenix Coyotes of the NHL. McNall, meanwhile, is still serving time in a U.S. prison for financial improprieties, while poor John Candy, one of our most beloved funnymen passed away in 1994 at the young age of 43.

28. By what name is Lim Kwong Yew better known?

A. Lim Kwong Yew became a CFL Hall of Famer under the professional name Normie Kwong. The China Clipper played 13 seasons in the league with Calgary and Edmonton. This tough halfback rushed for over 9,000 yards in his career, and was a pivotal member of the Edmonton Eskimos' powerhouse dynasty that won the 1954, 1955, and 1956 Grey Cups. A five-time all-star, this member of Canada's Sports Hall of Fame won two Schenley awards in his career.

Jackie Parker (left) and Normie Kwong

29. Who was known as "Ole Spaghetti Legs"?

A. Actually that was only one of Jackie Parker's nicknames, the other being The Fast Freight from Mississippi State. Parker had an outstanding CFL career dating back to 1954, when he was a member of the Edmonton Eskimos team that won three consecutive Grey Cups from 1954 to 1956. A versatile player, Parker starred as a quarterback, halfback, and defensive back. After retiring at the end of 1968 as a member of the B.C. Lions, he turned to coaching in 1969 with the same Lions, and went over to Edmonton Eskimos in 1983–87. This Hall of Famer won the Schenley Award three times, and was a CFL all-star on eight occasions.

30. How many Canadians have been inducted into the Pro Football Hall of Fame in Canton, Ohio?

A. As far as we can tell there's only been two of our boys who have made it to the American hall. One was Bronko Nagurski, who was born in Rainy River, Ontario, and grew up mostly in International Falls, Minnesota. He played nine seasons with the Chicago Bears as a rough and tough fullback who gained over 4,000 yards rushing in his career. He was a league all-star three times before retiring in 1943 and concentrating on his career as a professional wrestler. Nagurski was inducted into the Hall in 1963.

The second Canadian enshrined in Canton was big Arnie Weinmeister, a six-foot-four, 240-pound defensive tackle born in Rhein, Saskatchewan in 1923. Playing for the New York Giants, this four-time league all-star was considered by many to be one of the dominant tackles of his time. Weinmeister was inducted into the Hall of Fame in 1984.

31. Who has scored the most career points in the Canadian Football league?

A. Vancouver's own Lui Passaglia scored 3,991 points during his 25 year career. A graduate of Simon Fraser University, this local boy was a first round pick of the B.C. Lions in the 1976 draft. The leader in both seasons and games played along with total points scored, Passaglia holds over a dozen regular season and playoff kicking records in his career.

32. What high-profile Canadian quarterback was chosen by the New York Giants in the 2001 NFL draft?

A. Nepean, Ontario-raised Jesse Palmer had a rollercoaster career quarterbacking for the University of Florida Gators. This six-foot-two son of a former Ottawa Rough Rider was the victim of an unorthodox QB platoon system under head coach Steve Spurrier and a rash of injuries throughout his career. He nevertheless impressed enough scouts with his strong arm and physical attributes to be chosen in the fourth round of the 2001 draft. In his four years with the Gators, he played a total of 26 games, completing 260 passes for 31 touchdowns.

33. Does the Arena Football League have any teams in Canada?

A. It was in the year 2000 that a group of businessmen Rob Godfrey, Keith Stein, and Ronnie Strasser started the ball rolling in bringing this exciting high-scoring indoor form of pro football to the city of Toronto. By the late summer of that year, a deal had been signed to purchase and relocate the New England Sea Wolves. Their hard work was rewarded when on April 14, 2001, The Toronto Phantoms made their home debut at the Air Canada Centre, losing an exciting 61–54 decision to their cross-lake opponents, the Buffalo Destroyers.

34. What do actor Carl Weathers and wrestlers Lex Luger, Tito Santana, and Hacksaw Jim Duggan all have in common?

A. All the above gentlemen at one time or another had playing stints in the CFL.

35. Did an American network televise and showcase Canadian Football League games in the 1950s?

A. Yes, according to the book 505 *Television Questions Your Friend Can't Answer*. It happened in 1954, after ABC signed on to show several NCAA college football games and the now defunct DuMont network contracted to showcase NFL games. NBC, in an effort to stay competitive, committed itself to presenting Canadian professional football to the American public. The ratings were good, but American sponsors were unwilling to advertise during telecasts of a non-American product, and the network dropped the games. It would be another 30 years before the football-hungry American public would again be watching the CFL — in 1985 CFL games were broadcast in the U.S. during the NFL players' strike.

HOCKEY

1. Which one of these Montreal Canadiens was never a captain of the team?

a. Henri Richard
b. Yvon Cournoyer
c. Doug Harvey
d. Guy Lafleur

A. Even though he was one of the greatest superstars to ever lace up skates for the Canadiens, Guy Lafleur joins such notables as Elmer Lach, Boom Boom Geoffrion, Ken Dryden, and Dickie Moore as legends who never wore the "C" for Les Habs.

2. Who scored the first goal in WHA regular season history?

A. The renegade league that changed the face and business of hockey started its inaugural season in October 1972, and the first goal scored came off the stick of Ron Anderson of the Alberta (soon to be Edmonton) Oilers. This native of Red Deer, Alberta, played parts of six seasons in the NHL with the Red Wings, Kings, Blues, and Sabres before playing his last two in the WHA.

3. What was the first U.S. team to join the NHL?

A. The NHL, which formed in 1917, expanded into the United States for the first time in 1924 when it awarded the city of Boston its franchise and the big, bad Bruins were born. The franchise fee back in those days was only $15,000.

4. Who shot the puck that eliminated the Edmonton Oilers from the 1985–86 playoffs against the Calgary Flames?

A. Steven Smith shot the puck that banked off Edmonton Oiler goalie Grant Fuhr's leg, making him a hero for the Calgary Flames. He would have truly basked in the glory of the entire moment if it wasn't for the fact that he was a member of the Edmonton Oilers.

5. Did the late great Rocket Richard ever coach professional hockey?

A. Yes he did, albeit for a very brief time. When the WHA started up in 1972, the Quebec Nordiques thought it would be a natural to sign up French Canada's greatest sports icon to lead their team. But when the season started it was obvious that Richard was miserable and didn't want to move from Montreal to Quebec City. So just a few days into the season, the Rocket retired with a record of 1 win and 1 loss behind the bench.

Maurice "The Rocket" Richard

6. Who was the first Russian to be elected to the Hockey Hall of Fame?

A. No, it wasn't Vladislav Tretiak, though the Soviet goalie is in the Hall. Even before Tretiak, Anotoli Tarasov, the genius and architect of the Soviet hockey system, was inducted into the Hockey Hall of Fame. Tarasov retired in 1972 after winning another gold medal at the Sapporo Olympics, and coming out of retirement briefly in 1987 to act as special coaching consultant for the Vancouver Canucks. He was inducted into the Hall in 1974.

7. In the comedy classic *Wayne's World*, what was the name of the restaurant that Wayne and his buds hung out in?

A. In this hilarious movie, Wayne and the boys hung out at Stan Mikita's Donuts — named after the slick centreman of the Chicago Blackhawks. Mikita was a Hall of Famer who won two scoring championships and too many awards to list here before his retirement after the 1979–80 season. The naming of Stan Mikita's by the movie's star and writer Mike Myers was a tongue-in-cheek reference to a certain chain of Canadian donut shops named after another NHL all-star.

8. Mix and match the hockey player to the way in which he met his demise.

A. Tim Horton	a. Influenza
B. Terry Sawchuk	b. Plane crash
C. Joe Hall	c. Roughhousing with a teammate
D. Bill Barilko	d. Car accident
E. George Vezina	e. Tuberculosis

A. A-d, B-c, C-a, D-b, E-e

9. Which one of these hockey greats never won the Calder Trophy, awarded to the NHL Rookie of the Year?

a. Mario Lemieux
b. Bobby Orr
c. Wayne Gretzky
d. Ray Bourque

A. c. Wayne Gretzky. The NHL ruled that since he had played pro hockey in the WHA in 1978–79, he could not be classified as a rookie when he made his debut in the NHL the following year. The Calder Trophy that year went to Ray Bourque, and was one of the few awards Gretzky missed out on during his career.

Wayne Gretzky

10. What was the reason for the playing of the very first NHL All-Star Game on February 14, 1933?

A. The very first All-Star Game was organized to raise money for Toronto Maple Leaf left winger Ace Bailey, who was critically injured by the Boston Bruins' tough defenceman Eddie Shore. Even though doctors were able to save Bailey's life, his playing days were over. At the game, Bailey and Shore met for the first time since the incident and shook hands to a standing ovation from the crowd at Maple Leaf Gardens.

11. Did Maurice Richard ever win an NHL scoring title?

A. Surprisingly, no. He was among the league leaders many times throughout his spectacular career and was the first to score 50 goals in as many games, but the actual scoring title eluded the fiery Rocket. The closest he came was in the 1954–55 season when, with only a few games left, he was in a neck-and-neck race with his teammate Boom Boom Geoffrion. Then, the Rocket was suspended from all remaining games, including playoffs, after he struck an official. (Habs fans' anger over this suspension resulted in the infamous Richard Riot.) While Richard sat out the suspension, Geoffrion passed him to become scoring champion that season.

12. Who won more games between the pipes for the Montreal Canadiens, Jacques Plante or Ken Dryden?

A. Plante wins, only by a small margin. Including playoffs, Plante won a total of 370 games, followed closely by Dryden with a total of 338 wins.

13. Which one of these players was not a captain of the Toronto Maple Leafs?

a. George Armstrong
b. Frank Mahovlich
c. Wendel Clark
d. Rick Vaive

A. b. Frank Mahovlich, or "The Big M" as he was fondly known, broke into the NHL during the 1957–58 season, and beat out another rookie superstar by the name of Bobby Hull for the Rookie of the Year Award. A perennial all-star, Mahovlich scored 533 career goals and won six Stanley Cups, but he was never captain of the Maple Leafs.

14. They say that athletes are tough, but you don't often hear about some of the injuries suffered by officials during games. Is it true that an NHL official played through almost an entire game with a broken arm?

A. Darn right it's true, but you wouldn't expect any less from long-time NHL linesman John D'Amico, who was one of the strongest guys to ever lace on a pair of skates. A veteran of over 1,700 games, one of his most memorable came in 1982 when an errant puck struck D'Amico on the arm. He played through the resulting pain, then after the game, when he had the arm x-rayed, discovered that it was broken. After retiring in 1988, he went to work for the NHL as an officials coach.

15. Who was the only brother tandem to win the NHL scoring title?

A. It's a pretty safe bet that Max and Doug Bentley were the biggest thing to ever come out of Delisle, Saskatchewan. The slight, quick-skating brothers' puck control skills rank up there with the best ever. And yes, both of them won the scoring title, with older brother Doug winning in 1942–43 and Max winning twice, in 1944–45 and 1945–46.

16. What former NHL star released his own Christmas record?

A. Johnny Bower was born John Kishkin in Prince Albert, Saskatchewan (Bower is his step-father's last name). A four-time Stanley Cup winner, the "China Wall" turned recording star in 1965 with the release of the corny but catchy holiday tune, "Honky the Christmas Goose." Let's hope that goose was cooked the first time around.

17. Who was the youngest player ever to lace up his skates in the NHL?

A. Because of a shortage of players during the Second World War, quite a few players who normally weren't quite ready for the big leagues were called into service to bolster depleted rosters. The youngest of these was Aldo "Bep" Guidolin, who in 1942–43 made his NHL debut at the ripe old age of 16. He ended up playing almost ten years in the league, and in later years became a head coach for the Bruins.

18. Did an active NHL player ever hold a political office?

A. A number of athletes have held political office, but on only two occasions did an NHL star do so while still an active player. The first hockey-playing politician was former Rookie of the Year Howie Meeker, who served as the Conservative MP for Waterloo from 1951–53. A decade later, perennial all-star Red Kelly served as the Liberal member of Parliament for York-West from 1962–65. Coincidentally, the Conservative candidate Kelly defeated to win the seat was a young lawyer by the name of Alan Eagleson.

19. In the famous story "The Hockey Sweater," who did author Roch Carrier want to be?

A. If you haven't read the story then you've probably seen the animated short film. In this tale a young boy's dream of being Maurice Richard turns into a nightmare when he's forced by his mother to wear a Toronto Maple Leafs jersey while playing shinny in rural Quebec.

20. How long did Don Cherry actually play in the NHL?

A. As a player, Don Cherry was a tough-minded physical defenceman who toiled in the American Hockey League for 20 years. Only once did Cherry make it all the way to the NHL, and then it was only for one game. On March 31, 1955, Grapes suited up for the Boston Bruins in a 5–1 loss to the Montreal Canadiens. After retiring, coached in the AHL, before achieving fame as the head coach of first the Bruins, and then the short-lived Colorado Rockies. After his coaching days were over, Cherry turned his eye towards the TV camera, and the rest is history.

21. Can you match the hockey player to his colourful nickname?

A. Big Bird	a. George Armstrong
B. Busher	b. Guy Lafleur
C. Killer	c. Larry Robinson
D. Chief	d. Harvey Jackson
E. The Flower	e. Doug Gilmour

A. A-c, B-d, C-e, D-a, E-b

22. Who scored the last goal at Maple Leaf Gardens?

A. Even with her tight seats and horrible parking, there was something magical about The Grand Old Lady of Hockey. It was with sadness that the last game was played at Maple Leaf Gardens on February 13, 1999, when the Leafs lost to Chicago 6–2. The last goal in the Gardens was scored by the Hawks' Bob Probert.

23. What New Brunswick native won both the NHL scoring title and the Lady Byng award?

A. Gordie Drillon of Moncton, New Brunswick, broke in with the Leafs in the 1936–37 season with the unenviable task of temporarily replacing the injured Charlie Conacher. He proved himself to be one of the most prolific goal scorers of the era, potting 155 goals in a short career that spanned a mere seven seasons. The 1937–38 season was perhaps his most memorable, earning him the NHL scoring title and the Lady Byng Trophy, awarded to the player who best combines sportsmanship and skill.

24. What former Maple Leaf defenceman is now employed as a television sportscaster?

A. Jim "Howie" McKenny was one of the most colourful characters to ever have donned the blue and white of the Maple Leafs. Being a partyer of world class proportions it's a wonder that he was able to fit ten full seasons into his social calendar. After retiring as a Minnesota North Star after the 1978–79 season, he caught on at a local radio station and began to teach himself every aspect of broadcasting, be it behind the mike or camera or in the editing room. He soon moved on to become an outstanding sportscaster at Toronto's City TV.

25. What was it that Harry "Moose" Watson did for a living after leaving his home of St. John's, Newfoundland?

A. Even though he never turned pro, Harry Watson was known as one of the finest all-around hockey players of the 1920s and early 1930s. In fact, his services were so much in demand that he was offered $30,000 a year to turn pro for the Montreal Maroons, a king's ransom for the times. Watson turned down the offer in order to remain eligible for the Olympics. Watson won two Allan Cups in his illustrious career and was named outstanding player on the 1924 gold medal Olympic team. This proud Newfoundlander was inducted into the Hockey Hall of Fame in 1962.

26. What P.E.I. native was coach and GM of both the Colorado Rockies and the New Jersey Devils?

A. Billy MacMillan was born in Charlottetown in 1943 and took to the ice at an early age. He became a member of the national team in 1966, then turned pro in 1970 with the Toronto Maple Leafs. MacMillan went on to play for the Atlanta Flames before closing his career with the New York Islanders in 1977. After retiring, MacMillan went behind the bench as a coach and GM with the Colorado Rockies and, after the move out east, the New Jersey Devils.

27. April 16, 1999, was a sad day for all Canadian sports fans. What happened?

A. This was the day that Wayne Gretzky announced that he was going to retire from hockey. A list of the Great One's accomplishments would take up half this book — he amassed 61 records during a career that started in the 1978–79 season and ended with his last game against the Penguins on April 18, 1999.

28. When was the first NHL game played?

A. There are actually two answers to this question. The first regular season game in league history saw the Montreal Wanderers defeat the Toronto Arenas 10–9 on December 19, 1917. Four days prior to this first official game, however, an exhibition was played between the Montreal Maroons and the Montreal Wanderers. The game was a benefit organized to aid victims of the horrific Halifax explosion, which had occurred a couple of weeks earlier, killing more than 1,600 people, injuring 9,000 and leaving 6,000 homeless.

29. Which NHL hockey player got his start in the public eye wrestling a bear?

A. It was in 1949 and Marcel Bonin, a sixteen-year-old teenager from Quebec, went with friends to the Barnum & Bailey Circus in Montreal. One of the acts featured former world heavyweight boxing champion Joe Louis fighting a muzzled and declawed four hundred-pound bear. When they asked if anyone in the crowd had the guts to challenge the beast, only young Marcel stepped forward. In fact, he did so well that he went on tour with the circus wrestling the bear, but left to pursue his hockey career. Bonin broke in with the Detroit Red Wings in 1952–53 and was traded to the Canadiens. He was part of four Stanley Cup winning teams in Montreal and played right-wing in five All-Star games.

30. What NHL team is in the record books for having the fewest victories in league history?

A. This dubious honour goes to the Montreal Wanderers in the league's first season in 1917. The Wanderers won their first game, beating the Toronto Arenas 10–9, but lost their next five games and were having trouble attracting fans. Then on January 2, 1918, the Westmount Arena, which the Wanderers shared with the Montreal Maroons, burnt down, taking with it all the team equipment. The Maroons moved temporarily to a smaller arena, but the after some thought, Wanderers executives decided to shut down the entire franchise, leaving the team with only one NHL victory in its very brief existence. On the bright side, they also posted the fewest losses in league history.

31. Who scored the first regular season goal in NHL history?

A. The very first goal in NHL history was scored on opening night December 19, 1917, by Montreal Wanderers defenceman Dave Richie (he scored two that evening) when they defeated the Toronto Arenas 10–9.

32. Name the hockey family that produced three generations of the sport's most recognizable journalists and broadcasters?

A. The Hewitts are legends in the sport of hockey. W.A. (William Atraham) Hewitt was the sports editor of *The Toronto Star* for 31 years, and was the long-time secretary of the Ontario Hockey Association. His son, Foster, who pioneered hockey broadcasting, and was the first to call a hockey game on March 22, 1923, out of Toronto's Mutual Street Arena. Late in his career, Foster was joined in the broadcast booth by his son Bill, who would eventually step out on his own and succeed his father as the voice of Canadian hockey.

33. Who won the gold medal in hockey at the 1936 Olympics?

A. For a while after hockey's first appearance as an Olympic sport in the 1920 Antwerp Games, Canada thoroughly dominated the competition. Up to the 1936 games, Canada had played

16 Olympic matches, winning all of them and outscoring the opposition 209–8. So it was a great shock when Canada was defeated 2–1 by Great Britain in the gold medal game, leaving the shocked Canucks with a mere silver.

34. Who was the only defenceman ever to win the scoring title?

A. Bobby Orr was arguably the greatest hockey player ever to lace on a pair of skates. In just nine NHL seasons, this Parry Sound native was league MVP three times, an all-star in every season he played, and the winner a plethora of awards from the Conn Smythe to the Lou Marsh. But the accomplishment that really sticks out is his two NHL scoring titles. No defenceman before or since has ever topped the league in points. Unfortunately, however, Orr's career was cut short. After a number of serious knee injuries, he retired in 1978. Orr is currently a businessman and player agent based in the U.S.

35. What does the date September 28, 1972, mean to Canadian hockey fans?

A. It's the day that will be remembered forever in Canadian history as the day Paul Henderson scored to lead Team Canada to a 6–5 win over the Soviet Union in the deciding game of the first ever Canada-USSR hockey series. Henderson achieved hero status for scoring the most famous goal in the history of the sport. But what is sometimes forgotten is that Henderson not only scored the winner in that game, but also in the last three games in the hockey showdown.

36. Which hockey family has bred three generations of NHL players?

Paul Henderson and Team Canada 1972

A. If you picked the Hextalls from the province of Manitoba then you'd be correct. It all started with grandfather Bryan Sr., who broke into the league in 1936 and had terrific success, winning a scoring title and being voted to the all-star team before retiring in 1948. Next Bryan's sons Bryan Jr. and Dennis made their marks in the league. Bryan Jr. was a very steady and travelled centreman who played on five different NHL teams before his exit from the game after the 1975–76 season. Dennis, meanwhile, broke into the NHL in 1968–69, and had stints with the Rangers, North Stars, Red Wings, and Capitals before retiring in 1980. And most recently, Bryan Jr.'s son Ron was a fiery goalie who spent most of his career with the Philadelphia Flyers where he won the 1987 Conn Smythe award and is the only goalie to have scored two goals in the league.

37. Who was the first black player to appear in the NHL?

A. Willie O'Ree of Fredericton, New Brunswick, opened the door to equality on January 18, 1958, when he helped the Boston Bruins defeat the Montreal Canadiens 3–0. O'Ree never became a full-time player, appearing in only two games in 1958 and another 43 in 1960–61. He had a very successful and lengthy career in the minors where he played until retiring after the 1978–79 season.

38. Which team name has been around in the NHL longer, the Toronto Maple Leafs or the Montreal Canadiens?

A. The Leafs and the Habs have one of the oldest rivalries in professional sports. And here's some more fuel to heat up the grudge. The oldest name is held by the Montreal Canadiens, who can trace their name back to the NHA (National Hockey Association), which was the forerunner of the NHL when the team was established in 1911. The Toronto

Maple Leafs weren't named such until after Conn Smythe pur-
chased the Toronto St. Pats in the 1927–28 season and renamed them The Leafs.

39. Who assisted on Paul Henderson's goal in the eighth game of the Canada-Russia series?

A. Phil Esposito, Team Canada's leader on and off the ice, got the assist on that memorable goal. This multi-time winner of the NHL scoring title potted two goals of his own in that final game to make for a total of seven that he scored in the series.

40. Was there ever a professional hockey league in the Maritimes?

A. After the turn of the last century there was a huge boom in the sport of hockey, with new leagues being formed all over Canada. The Maritimes were no exception when in 1910 the Interprovincial Hockey League was formed in Nova Scotia. In the 1911–12 season the league expanded and was renamed The Maritime Hockey League with teams representing cities like Halifax, Moncton, Glace Bay, Sydney, and North Glasgow. Alas, the league floundered, and after trying to hang on as the three-team Eastern Professional Hockey League in 1914–15, it was folded on February 7, 1915.

41. How many Gretzkys played in the NHL?

A. There was more than just one hockey-playing son from the Gretzkys of Brantford, Ontario. Wayne's oldest brother Keith was drafted 56th overall by the Buffalo Sabres in 1985, but never got out of the minor leagues. He went on to a career as a coach, most recently with the Ashville Smoke of the United Hockey League. Another brother, Brent, was picked 49th overall in the 1992 draft by the Tampa Bay Lightning and played a handful of games in the NHL. Unfortunately, Brent's final NHL stats came up a little short of Wayne's: he scored a total of one NHL goal.

42. Which NHL team were the Nova Scotia Voyageurs a farm club for?

A. The Voyageurs of the American Hockey League were the long-time farm club of the Montreal Canadiens, feeding them fantastic players who would help guide the Habs to Stanley Cup dominance in the 1970s. From the 1971–72 season to 1984, the Voyageurs introduced such notables as Larry Robinson, Chris Nilan, Richard Sevigny, and Wayne Thomas to the league. After the 1984 season, the Edmonton Oilers took over the AHL's maritime representative, renaming them the Nova Scotia Oilers.

43. What song about a Toronto Maple Leaf forward made the charts in Canada?

A. In 1966, "Clear the Track Here Comes Shack," a humorous ditty about the colourful life of Eddie "The Entertainer" Shack, hit the airwaves, and reached number one on CHUM radio's charts in Toronto. The song was written by well-known hockey author and broadcaster Brian McFarlane, and was performed by Douglas Rankine and the Secrets. Shack, a seventeen-year veteran of the NHL, may have been the clown prince of pro hockey, but he was also a pretty good hockey player, scoring a total of 239 goals in his lengthy career.

44. Which Canadian team joined the NHL in the 1970–71 season?

A. By the late 1960s it became evident that NHL's six-team expansion in 1967–68 had been such a success that further expansion would be possible. And so, on May 22, 1970, the league awarded franchises to Buffalo and Vancouver, giving Canada its third NHL team.

45. Has an NHL player ever died from an injury sustained during a game?

A. On January 13, 1969, a twenty-nine year old, Minnesota North Stars forward by the name of Bill Masterton got sandwiched between two other players while leading a rush during a game against the Oakland Seals. His head hit the ice and he was rushed to the hospital, but succumbed to his injuries two days later. The ironic thing about this entire tragedy was that Masterton had actually quit playing hockey a few years earlier. After a stint in the minor leagues, he had gotten fed up trying to break into the NHL and went back to school, receiving a masters degree from Denver University and going to work with Honeywell Inc. When the NHL expanded for the 1967–68 season, there was a larger market for players and Bill took one more shot at the brass ring.

After his death, the NHL donated an award named after their fallen comrade to be given out to the player that best exemplifies perseverance, sportsmanship, and dedication to hockey.

46. Who has won more NHL scoring titles, Wayne Gretzky or Mario Lemieux?

A. Wayne Gretzky won ten scoring titles including, an incredible seven consecutive wins from 1981–1987. Lemieux, who's no slouch himself won a total of six scoring titles in his career before being forced into early retirement due to back injuries and a disdain for the goonism that he felt was hurting the game. In 2001, Lemieux came out of retirement, though it would take quite an effort to close in on the Great One's record.

47. One brother won the Norris Trophy as the NHL's best defenceman. The other won a Schenley Award as football's outstanding Canadian. Who are they?

A. Harry and Ron Howell were two of the finest athletes to ever come out of the city of Hamilton, Ontario. After a great junior hockey career, Harry caught on with the NHL's New York Rangers in 1952–53 and stayed there for the next 21 seasons. This stalwart player was named captain of the New York Rangers and in 1967 won the Norris Trophy the year before the great Bobby Orr took a stranglehold on the award.

Ron Howell was a pretty fair hockey player himself, and had a brief NHL career with the same New York Rangers. But it was in the sport of football that he really excelled, starring in college for the McMaster Marauders and then for the CFL's Hamilton Tiger-Cats. In 1958, Ron was awarded a Schenley award as the outstanding Canadian, and then scored two touchdowns in the Grey Cup for the Ti-Cats, only to see his team lose the cup 35–28 to the Winnipeg Blue Bombers.

48. Which Canadian athlete made a one-time guest appearance on the soap opera "The Young and the Restless"?

A. 1981–82 was quite a year for Wayne Gretzky. Along with shattering just about every scoring record with his 92-goal 212-point season, he was awarded the Hart Trophy, the Art Ross Trophy, the Lester Pearson Award, and The Sporting News Most Valuable Athlete Award. Unfortunately Wayne was unable to earn a Daytime Emmy for his forgettable appearance on "The Young and the Restless."

49. Who did Wayne Gretzky pass to become the most prolific scorer in NHL history?

A. It was the pride of Floral, Saskatchewan, Gordie Howe. Gordie made his NHL debut in 1946, playing for the Detroit Red Wings until his "first" retirement after the 1970–71 season.

Gordie Howe

After a couple of years, the restless Howe came out of retirement and signed with the WHA's Houston Aeros, and then went to the New England Whalers. There Howe earned another place in the history books by becoming a teammate of his two sons, Marty and Mark. After the WHA folded and the Whalers switched leagues, Gordie found himself in the NHL again. He finally ended his playing career — sort of — after the 1979–80 season with 1,767 NHL games to his credit, having scored 802 goals, and 1,048 assists. But, as it turned out, he wasn't done yet. On October 3, 1997, at the age of 69, he came out of retirement to skate one shift for the Detroit Vipers of the International Hockey League, allowing him to claim to have played professional hockey in six different decades.

50. Is it true that Peter Pocklington won the rights to negotiate a hockey deal with Wayne Gretzky in a card game?

A. According to the book A Concise History of Sport in Canada (Oxford University Press), sports entrepreneur Nelson

Skalbania, who owned the WHA Indianapolis Racers, signed Wayne Gretzky to his first pro contract in 1978 when the Great One was only 17. Having problems putting people in the seats, Skalbania was feeling the financial crunch and it's said that during a card game rival WHA owner Peter Pocklington of the Edmonton Oilers won the right to negotiate a change of teams for Wayne Gretzky, who signed with the Oilers for a reported $800,000.

51. What former NHL star is currently a member of the Canadian senate?

A. Frank Mahovlich was born in Timmins, Ontario, and showed signs of being a potential NHL talent from a young age. A graduate of the St. Mikes hockey program, he joined the Maple Leafs in 1958 and went on to win the Calder Trophy as the league's top rookie. His twenty-year career saw him score 533 goals and play integral role in six Stanley Cup wins, four of them with the Leafs and with the Montreal Canadiens. After his retirement, Mahovlich entered the business world with substantial success in travel. In 1998, he was chosen to sit in the Canadian Senate.

52. Who was the first NHL goalie to wear a mask?

A. Though it may surprise some, the answer is not Jacques Plante. In fact, it was Clint Benedict of the Montreal Maroons who briefly tried the mask 30 years earlier. During the 1929–30 season Canadiens star Howie Morenz bounced a shot off the probiscus of Benedict, and the thirteen-year NHL vet decided to try the leather constructed shield. But he never felt comfortable with the mask, and soon abandoned it. It would be another 30 years before Plante wore a mask of his own. This time the idea stuck, and the goalie mask became a permanent part of the game.

53. What member of the clergy was a driving force behind international hockey in Canada?

A. Father David Bauer was born in Kitchener, Ontario, into a large sports-minded family that included his older brother Bob, who was a member of the famous Kraut line of the Boston Bruins. David himself was a talented hockey player who in 1943 was a member of the Oshawa hockey team that won the Memorial Cup. Foregoing a pro career to join the priesthood, Father David, as he was called, put together an standing amateur national team for international competitions. A coach and educator at St. Michael's College, and then St. Mark's and the University of British Columbia, this sports Hall of Famer had a lot to do with the moulding of not only great athletes but of fine young men.

54. What Canadian sports star was immortalized in song by music superstars The Tragically Hip?

A. The song "Fifty Mission Cap" tells the story of Toronto Maple Leaf defenceman Bill Barilko, the hero of the 1951 playoffs. The bruising defenceman was born in Timmins and joined the Maple Leafs in the 1946–47 season. In game five of the 1951 Stanley Cup final against the Montreal Canadiens, Barilko was on the ice in overtime. A devastating body checker not usually associated with goal scoring, Barilko became a surprise hero when he blasted the puck past Habs goalie Gerry MacNeil to win the cup for the Leafs. Later that summer, Barilko was killed in a small plane crash near his hometown of Timmins. The plane and Barilko's remains weren't found until 12 years later.

55. What Toronto Maple Leaf captain competed in the 1936 Olympics in track and field?

A. The Paris, Ontario-born Syl Apps was one of the finest all-around athletes in the country, having competed for Canada in track and field at the 1936 Olympics and captained the football team at his alma mater McMaster University in Hamilton. Professionally, he spent 13 years in the NHL as a member of the Toronto Maple Leafs, most of those years as team captain. In his rookie year, Apps became the first recipient of the Calder Trophy, given to the NHL's most impressive newcomer. He was a member of three Stanley Cup winners and five All-Star teams, and scored over 200 goals in his career. After his retirement, he was appointed Ontario Athletics Commissioner, and for a number of years was a Conservative member of the Ontario Parliament.

56. Who was responsible for the NHL's first players' union?

A. Ted Lindsay was one of the toughest all-around hockey players ever to play the game. Back in the mid-50s while a member of the Detroit Red Wings, Lindsay, with help from Montreal Canadiens star Doug Harvey, started the first players' union. Both were members of the NHL Pension Society Board and were quite upset at the team owners' refusals to give them league financial statements. It was a difficult fight as owners and team management people did everything they could to crush the new union. Union leaders and followers found themselves traded to bad teams, sent down to the minors, or benched. Both Lindsay and Harvey, though at the top of their games, both traded — Lindsay to the Blackhawks and Harvey to the Rangers. It was soon after Lindsay's trade that Red Wings players dropped out of the union, creating a domino effect that crushed Lindsay and Harvey's dream. It would be more than a decade before a union led by Alan Eagleson would take hold in the NHL.

57. Which NHL player has the distinction of winning the most Stanley Cups in his career?

A. Henri Richard, known to all as the "Pocket Rocket", and the kid brother of the famed Maurice Richard, won a grand total of 11 Stanley Cups in a career that spanned 20 seasons, from 1955–55 to 1974–75. This former Canadiens captain scored 358 goals in his career, and in ten All-Star games. In 1974, he was awarded the Bill Masterton Trophy, given to the player who best exhibits perseverance and sportsmanship.

Jean Beliveau and Gordie Howe

58. Who was affectionately known as Le Gros Bill?

A. Born in Trois Rivieres, Quebec, Jean Beliveau was a hockey sensation from a young age. A big man at 6'3" and over 200 pounds, he nevertheless was one of the greatest finesse players to play the game. By the time he played Junior "A" for the Quebec Aces, the Montreal Canadiens were so worried about someone else signing this phenom that they bought the entire league as an insurance policy. Beliveau rewarded the team for its confidence, for when he joined the big club in the 1953–54 season, he became not just one of the great players in the league but a team leader for the Canadiens. In eighteen seasons he scored a total of 507 goals, played on ten Stanley Cup winners, and was elected to the All-Star team ten times. After retiring, he became an executive for the Canadiens.

59. Who was the "Stratford Streak"?

A. The story of Howie Morenz is surely one of the most fascinating in the rich history of Canadian sports. The quintessential Montreal Canadien, he broke into the league during the 1923–24 season, and thrived for the next seventeen years. Playing at a time when scoring 20 goals in a fifty-game season was a major accomplishment, Morenz tallied 270 goals and 197 assists in 550 regular season games, while potting another 21 goals during the post-season, leading the Habs to three Cup wins. Morenz's career came to a tragic end when, on January 28, 1937, while being checked against the boards, he suffered a broken leg. It was clear to everyone that the injury was so severe it would signal the end of his career, but it came as a great shock to all when on March 8 of that year, while still recuperating from his injury, the great Morenz passed away at the young age of 34. The official cause of death was listed as heart failure, but most who knew him claim that without hockey his will just gave up.

60. Who has scored more total goals in their professional hockey careers, Bobby Hull or his son Brett?

A. Well, it all depends on whether you want to count Bobby's seven-year stint in the WHA. If you do, then Bobby comes out on top with, including playoffs, a 1,018 goals in his impressive twenty-four-year career. Brett, in his sixteen-year NHL career up to the end of the 2001 season, has amassed 739 regular season and playoff goals, well back of his father's totals. But if you exclude Bobby's WHA totals then you have a much closer race, with Brett coming out on top 739 to 672 in roughly the same number of seasons played.

61. What Canadian national team sports a perfect 35–0 record in world championship play?

A. Right up to and including the 2001 world championships, our Canadian Women's Hockey Team has dominated the sport for the better part of the past decade, winning seven straight world championships and compiling a perfect 35–0 record. Players such as Manon Rheume, Cassie Campbell, Geraldine Heaney, and Hayley Wickenheiser have become household names as the team's successes on the ice have captured the hearts of Canadians in big numbers. Unfortunately, in 1998 at the Nagano Winter Games, where women's hockey was making its Olympic debut, our heavily favoured Canadian team was defeated by the U.S. squad in the finals and our gals had to settle for the silver medal.

62. What was Herb Carnegie stopped from accomplishing in his stellar athletic career?

A. Herb Carnegie was one of the best hockey players to never play in the NHL. Playing in the Quebec Senior League — one of the major talent pools that supplies many future stars to the NHL — Herb Carnegie was one of those players that most scouts agreed should be a shoe-in to make it to the pros. The problem was that Herb was black. Born to Jamaican parents in Toronto in 1919, Carnegie was victim to the blatant racial discrimi-nations that were typical of not just sports, but of all aspects of society at the time. Herb played on a line with brothers Ossie and

Manny McIntyre, and together they comprised an all-black line that was one of the most dominant trios of the time. Several NHL teams expressed interest in signing Herb, including the Toronto Maple Leafs, but none were bold enough to break the NHL colour line. Leaf boss Conn Smythe was reportedly quoted as saying he would give anyone $10,000 if they could make Herb Carnegie white. A decade later, Willie O'Ree would become the first black player in the league when he joined the Boston Bruins.

63. Who set the NHL record of scoring ten points in a single NHL game?

A. Born just outside Kitchener, Ontario, Darryl Sittler would become one of the greatest players to ever play for the Toronto Maple Leafs. While he had many great moments in his career, his most memorable came on the night of February 7, 1976, when Sittler exploded for six goals and four assists in an 11–4 Leaf victory over the Boston Bruins. The performance established a record that still stands 25 years later. The classy Sittler remains on the team as a special Leaf community and alumni ambassador.

64. Did a team from the Yukon ever challenge for the Stanley Cup?

A. Yes. Back in 1905, years before the NHL came into being, the Stanley Cup was a challenge trophy open to just about any hockey team in Canada. The champions at the time were the Ottawa Silver Seven, who were the Cup's first dynasty retaining the trophy for four straight years. In late 1904, Ottawa accepted a challenge from the Dawson City Nuggets, and invited them to make the 6,000 kilometre journey to the nation's capital to start the two game series on January 13, 1905. The team left the Yukon on December 19, 1904, and faced a daunting journey. They were forced to walk and bicycle the first 200 miles through a freezing blizzard, dog sled for another good clip, and then travel by boat to Seattle, Washington. From there they took a train all the way across Canada to Ottawa. Arriving exhausted after 23 days of continuous travelling, the Nuggets caught the imagination of hockey fans everywhere, and were cheered wherever they went. But when it came down to the actual games, the exhausted Nuggets were no match for the Silver Seven, who destroyed the challengers from the Yukon in both games, 9–2 and 23–2.

65. Harold Ballard and Alan Eagleson had more in common than a mutual love of hockey. Both gentlemen were found guilty of unrelated fraud and theft charges. Ballard in 1972 and Eagleson in 1998. Who spent longer incarcerated for their deeds?

A. On October 20, 1972, Harold Ballard was sentenced by Judge Jarry Deyman to a prison term of three years, but the Leaf owner was paroled after serving 364 days. Eagleson was sentenced to an eighteen-month term on January 7, 1998, of which he served only six months. That means our pal Hal spent approximately twice as long inside as The Eagle.

HORSES

1. Did a member of the current Royal Family ever compete in the Olympics?

A. The Royal Family, who have a reputation for being sportspersons, were thrilled when Princess Anne qualified to represent Britain in the Montreal Olympics as a member of the equestrian team. Anne's siblings and parents were all on hand to watch the competition, marking this the first time the entire immediate Royal Family was in Canada together. Princess Anne finished 24th in a field of 30.

2. Which jockey was the first Canadian to win 500 races in a season?

A. Oshawa's Sandy Hawley achieved this feat. Sandy's career began in 1968 when he was named Rookie of the Year. In 1970, he set a Canadian record of 485. He then set his sights on

500, reaching the mark in 1973. That same year Hawley received the Lou Marsh Award as Canada's Athlete of the Year.

3. Who was the first woman to win horse racing's Sovereign Award, symbolic of Canada's Rookie of the Year?

A. This accomplishment belongs to Valerie Thompson of Port Colborne, Ontario, who in 1980 became the first female jockey to be awarded the prestigious honour. A tomboy from childhood, this petite but gutsy athlete not only excelled on top of a horse, but also in between the pipes as a hockey goaltender. She showed everyone what a talent she was when, in 1980, she had 89 first place finishes to win the award. She was always a steady competitor, and continued her success after her move to the U.S. in the early 1980s. However, her career suffered a serious setback in 1987 when she was involved in a serious accident in which she shattered her arm, broke one of her feet, and six ribs. Despite showing incredible courage by returning to horse racing, she was never quite the same as before her injuries, and Thompson took a long break from the sport in 1993.

4. What famous horse ran his last race right here in Canada?

A. The Canadian International was one of the most respected and distinguished annual events not only here in Canada, but worldwide. In fact next to the Newfoundland Regatta, it's the oldest sporting event in the country, dating back to 1860. The International has been host to many of the great horses of

Ron Turcotte

the past 150 years, but none was as big an attraction as the legendary Secretariat. In 1973, this elegant horse not only won the Triple Crown of racing, but he did so by smashing speed records wherever he went along the way. On Sunday October 28, 1973, this legendary animal made his last appearance on the track, winning the Canadian International by 6 1/2 lengths. The win came despite the fact that Secretariat was racing with a handicap: his regular jockey, Ron Turcotte of Canada, couldn't compete due to an earlier suspension.

5. What famous jockey was Taber, Alberta's favourite son?

A. Johnny Longden was considered by most horse racing experts to be one of the greatest jockeys of his time. In a thirty-nine year racing career that began in 1927, he rode 6,032 winners — a world record at the time. Longden won most of the top races of the day, but his biggest triumph came in 1943 when he won the Triple Crown of racing aboard Count Fleet. A tough competitor, he suffered many injuries, including a broken back and legs. His doctors advised him to give up horse racing on many occasions, but Longden always ignored them, and continued to race until his retirement in 1966.

6. Who in the sport of horse racing was known to his fans as "Gomey"?

A. Without a doubt Avelino Gomez was one of the most controversial, talented, and colourful riders to ever don the silks. Born in Cuba, he came to Canada as a young man in 1955, and began a career that saw him become the first rider to win the Queen's Plate four times. Gomez was chosen as Canada's finest jockey no less than eight times in his career, and in 1966 was named the top jockey in all of North America. Tragically, we lost Gomey in 1980 at Toronto's Woodbine racetrack when his mount,

Swisskin, buckled and fell, and the horse that was running behind them fell over and crushed the fallen jockey.

7. The bronze statue at the Santo Anita racetrack is in tribute to which Canadian jockey?

A. It was erected in memory of Cardston, Alberta's George Woolf. Nicknamed the "Iceman" for his cool headiness in tough races, Woolf was one of the top jockeys in North America throughout the 30s and early 40s. A careful man, he didn't accept nearly as many mounts as other jockeys, which kept him from riding as many winners as others had, yet twice in his career — in 1942 and 1944 — he was the top money maker in the sport. In 1936, he won the Preakness Stakes on Bold Venture, and in 1938 he rode what he considered his greatest mount, Seabiscuit, to a win over War Admiral in a special match race. Sadly, on January 3, 1946, at Santo Anita, Woolf's horse Please Me stumbled and threw Woolf to the ground. The rider received a fatal head injury. When the U.S. Jockey Hall of Fame opened its doors in 1955, the "Iceman" George Woolf was among the original trio of riders inducted.

8. What Canadian harness racer was the first to win 400 races in a season?

A. Hervé Fillion, born in Angers, Quebec, in 1940, came from a large, hardworking farm family. Not exactly enamoured with school, he began to frequent the local racetrack, eventually taking a job as a horse groomer there at 13. His terrific winning attitude has driven him to a plethora of awards and recognition as one of the world's greatest harness racers. He has been named driver of the year numerous times and has posted over 5,000 victories in his career. In 1968, he was the first harness racer to win over 400 races in a season, winning a record 407 races. He then broke his own record with 486 wins in 1970, and followed that with 543 wins in 1971 and an amazing 605 wins in 1972. Fillion was inducted into the Canadian Sports Hall of Fame in 1969.

9. At the time of this writing there has been only one athlete from the beautiful Prince Edward Island elected to Canada's Sports Hall of Fame. Can you name him?

A. Champion harness racer, pharmacist, newspaper publisher, war hero: it's hard to believe that all of the above are among the accomplishments of just one man. Daniel MacKinnon, born in Highland, P.E.I., in 1876, was known as the father of east coast harness racing. MacKinnon started his racing career quite late at the age of 36, but for years was one of the most consistent drivers in Canada. More than just a harness racer, though, he was also P.E.I.'s first registered pharmacist, having achieved his registration through a mail-order course. In the First World War, he was awarded the French Croix de guerre and took part in the defence of Vimy Ridge. MacKinnon was a wonder to all who knew him and he was still racing and training his horses at the age of 85. He was inducted into the Hall of Fame in 1957.

10. What sport did Ian Millar and Big Ben compete in?

A. Big Ben and his rider Ian Millar were probably the most successful equestrian team in Canadian history. The beautiful 17.3-hand chestnut was born in Belgium and brought to Canada by Millar in 1983. During their decade-long career together the two rode to two World Cup titles, two golds at the Pan-Am Games, and countless Canadian and Grand Prix titles. Ian Millar, originally from Halifax, has the distinction of being the only Canadian athlete to be chosen to compete in eight Olympics. Both Millar and Big Ben were inducted into the Canadian Sports Hall of Fame in 1996. Big Ben passed away on

December 11, 1999 at the age of 23 from colic, five years after his retirement from competition.

Ian Millar and Big Ben

11. In the world of horse racing, which jockey was known as "Slasher" by his fans and "Professor" by his fellow jockeys?

A. Ted Atkinson was definitely one of the top jockeys to ever come out of our country. Born in Toronto and raised in the U.S., Atkinson got a late start in the sport at age 20, and began his career racing in the small midwest circuit. Within a few years, he made it to New York and the major racetracks, and never left. He won the U.S. riding title twice, in 1944 and 1946. He rode more than 4,000 winners in his career, and won the 1949 Preakness and Belmont Stakes upon "Cabot."

12. Which Canadian businessman became the world's largest breeder of thoroughbred horses?

A. Born into a wealthy Ottawa banking family, Edward Plunket Taylor, better known to Canadians as E.P., was an extremely successful businessman who built a brewery empire and also organized the birth of the Argus Corporation, the first large Canadian holding company. But the true calling in his life was to the Sport of Kings, horse racing. As president of the Ontario Jockey Club from 1953–73, Taylor oversaw the modernization of facilities and the building of the state-of-the-art Woodbine Racetrack in Toronto. Much of his fame, though, came from the successes of his beloved horses, including the great Northern Dancer and Nijinsky. His horses won 15 Queen's Plates, and in 1973 he was named Man of the Year by the U.S. Thoroughbred Racing Association.

13. What Canadian business tycoon has become one of the most influential figures in the sport of horse racing?

A. Born in Austria and a Canadian since immigrating here in 1954, Frank Stronach is the model of a self-made man. Arriving in Canada almost penniless, he turned a one-man tool and dye operation into one of the largest makers of automatic components. His Magna Corp. sales exceed over $3 billion a year. A lifetime racehorse enthusiast, he has become one of the most successful racehorse owners and breeders, winning some of the most prestigious races in the world, including the 1997 Belmont Stakes and the 1998 Breeders Cup Classic. He has also turned to purchasing numerous racetracks, such as Santa Anita, Gulfstream, and Remington Park.

Track & Field

1. Canada did something that was pretty amazing in the 1900 Boston Marathon. What was it?

A. Amazing isn't a worthy enough superlative to describe the accomplishment and 1, 2, 3 finish of Canadians Jack Caffery, Bill Sherring, and Fred Hughson in the prestigious 26.2-mile race. Caffery, a native of Hamilton, Ontario, won the marathon again the next year.

2. Who was Ethel Catherwood, and what was her accomplishment for Canada?

A. At the 1928 Amsterdam Olympics, Catherwood became the first Canadian woman to win an Olympic gold medal. Fortunately she wasn't the last, though to some backwards-thinking people, she may have been. It was at those same Olympics that a movement emerged — led in part by the Canadian contingent —

to eliminate women's events from future Games. Competitive sports, it was argued, were physiologically and psychologically unsuitable for women. Thank goodness great athletes like Catherwood ignored such opinions and proved that they belonged on sports' biggest stage.

Ethel Catherwood

3. What was so unusual about the first gold medal ever won by a Canadian?

A. George Orton was born in Strathroy, Ontario, and was one of the greatest track runners of his time. In 1896, he went to Athens for the first modern Olympics and won the gold medal in the 2,500-metre steeplechase. Now for the unusual part: since Canada didn't send a team to those first Olympics, and an athlete had to have representation of a competing country, George won gold while running for the United States.

4. What spectacular feat did Percy Williams achieve for Canada?

A. Canada has had many track stars shine on the world scene. People like Donovan Bailey, Harry Jerome, Bruny Surin, and yes, even Ben Johnson. None could match what Percy Williams did and that was to win both the 100 and 200-metre sprints at the 1928 Amsterdam Olympics. It would be over 30 years before any Canadian would come close to matching Percy's racing accomplishment.

Harry Jerome

5. What Native Canadian distance runner became a national sports hero in the early part of the twentieth century?

A. Tom Longboat, born on the Six Nations reserve in 1887, won the 1907 Boston Marathon as well as dozens of other important races and challenge matches to become not only Canada's, but the world's, premier distance runner.

6. Who was Jacqueline Gareau?

A. Mademoiselle Gareau was the winner of the women's division of the 1980 Boston Marathon — a race that is, unfortunately, better remembered for who didn't win. This was the year that American Rosie Ruiz was initially thought to have won the event after she jumped into the race near the end without having run the entire course. A subsequent investigation revealed that Ruiz had cheated, and Gareau was declared the winner.

7. What world record did the Canadian Milers Club achieve on December 20, 1998?

A. The Milers Club set a world record by running 100 miles using 100 runners (one mile each) in an amazing time of 7 hours 35 minutes and 55.4 seconds — an average of 4 minutes, 33.6 seconds per runner. They must not have had a lot of runners in my league, 'cause if they did the competition would still be going on.

8. Who won the Boston Marathon of 1926?

A. It was generally thought that the 1926 Marathon was going to be a two-man race between Olympic champ Albin Stenroas and the winner of several past marathons, American

Clarence DeMor. So it was an absolute shock to all when Johnny Miles, a young twenty-one-year-old from Sydney Mines, Nova Scotia, came out of nowhere to not only win the race, but to do so in a world record time of 2 hours 25 minutes and 40 seconds. To prove that his win wasn't a fluke, Miles came back three years later, in 1929, to win again, setting another new record in the process.

Tom Longboat (middle row, fifth from left)
with the 1908 Canadian Olympic team

9. What was Fred Cameron's impressive achievement in the world of sports?

A. Canada has historically had tremendous success in the sport of marathon running, having produced such great athletes as Bill Sherring, Jerome Drayton, and Tom Longboat. Fred Cameron is another name that should be added to this list. Born in Amherst, Nova Scotia, he was another Canadian to do us proud when he won the Boston Marathon in 1910.

10. Who was the Canadian athlete who challenged a horse to an endurance race?

A. As hard as it may be to believe, famed Canadian marathoner Edouard Fabré challenged and raced a horse to see who could run further in 24 hours. And wouldn't you know it, the Montreal native bested his four-legged rival.

Fabré's endurance was legendary and his techniques were, to say the least, different. During a scheduled break at one endurance race, Fabré was found in a tent eating an apple pie and drinking a draft beer. As unconventional as he was, Fabré won literally hundreds of these races throughout his career, and in 1915 won the biggest race of his career, the Boston Marathon.

11. What was Mel Fitzgerald's sporting accomplishment for Canada?

A. Every so often you hear about one of those gifted humans who, despite handicaps or adversities, show the heart of a champion. Wheelchair competitor Mel Fitzgerald is one of these rare breeds and the Trepassey, Newfoundland native, amazed us all with his success on the track in the 1970s and 1980s. Winning a multitude of titles during his career, this worthy recipient of the Order of Canada highlighted his career by winning gold and silver in the 800 and 1,500-metre races at the 1980 Paralympics.

12. Who was Fanny Rosenfeld and what did she accomplish in Canadian sport?

A. The question should not be what did she accomplish, but what *didn't* she accomplish. This petite but wiry gal was one of the greatest all-around athletes ever produced in Canada — an all-star in hockey, baseball, basketball, and just about any sport that she ever tried. But it was in track and field that she had her greatest success. Rosenfeld represented Canada well on the international circuit, winning a silver medal in the 100-metre sprint and leading the 4x100-metre relay to a gold medal at the 1928 Olympics in Amsterdam. A few years later, stricken with arthritis, she retired from active competition and became a popular sports writer with the Toronto *Globe*.

13. What well-known Canadian track star began her athletic career masquerading a boy in an all-male hockey league?

A. In 1958, Abby Hoffman was just nine years old when, with her parents blessings, she cut her hair and joined an all-boys hockey league. A standout player, she impressed so much that when her little charade was uncovered she was asked to stay on the team. As she got a little older, Abby switched to track and field, where she found her niche as a middle distance runner. A stellar performer, her career was without parallel in the women's ranks as she competed in four Olympics (1964, 1968, 1972, and 1976), four Pan-Americans (1962, 1966, 1970, and 1974), three World University Games, and two Commonwealth Games (1971 and 1975). Since her retirement from competition, she has played a major role in helping Canadian athletes by promoting strong, innovative sports programs. She was also the Director General of Sport Canada, and most recently a senior advisor for the Women's Health Bureau.

14. Who presented the Queen with the ceremonial baton at the 1978 Commonwealth Games?

A. It was Diane Jones Konihowski who was given the honour at the opening of the 1978 Commonwealth Games in Edmonton, Alberta. Diane was born in Vancouver and raised in Saskatchewan. By the time she was in tenth grade, she was a national track and field team member and in 1976 finished sixth in the pentathlon at the Montreal Olympics. It was said that the pretty athlete was the most photographed competitor of the Games.

The winner of many championships, Diane won a gold medal at the 1978 Commonwealth Games to solidify her ranking as the number one female pentathlete in the world. She was chosen Canada's woman of the year twice, in 1975 and 1978. Now married to former CFL player John Konihowski, Diane balances raising a family with her work for amateur sports in Canada. Among her recent accomplishments was her role as the Chef de Mission for the Canadian contingent at the 2000 Sydney Games.

15. What 150-metre challenge race took place at Toronto's Sky Dome on June 1, 1997?

A. The events that led to this international challenge race began at the 1996 Olympics. American Michael Johnson won the 200-metre and 400-metre events at those Games, prompting NBC TV and *Sports Illustrated* to refer to Johnson as "The World's Fastest Man" an honour traditionally reserved for the winner of the 100-metre race — in this case, Canadian Donovan Bailey. The slighting of Bailey turned into a war of words between the two camps, culminating in the showdown in Toronto. Each sprinter was paid a $500,000 appearance fee, and would be racing for an additional purse of $1 million. With the eyes of the world on the two men, the race itself was one-sided and anti-climactic; Johnson, trailing in the race, suddenly came up lame and Bailey cruised to an easy victory and a record-setting $1.5 million windfall.

16. What important track event occurred in Vancouver's Empire Stadium on August 7, 1954?

A. Long before the Michael Johnson–Donovan Bailey challenge race of a few years back there was the "Mile of the

Century" race between Englishman Roger Bannister and Australian John Landy. Bannister had become the first man to ever run a sub-four-minute mile in a race in May of that year, only to have his mark bettered by Landy six weeks later. With the debate in the air over which runner was the fastest miler in the world, organizers put together the Vancouver race as part of the 1954 British Empire Games. Anyone who could watched on TV and over 35,000 people crammed into Empire Stadium. Landy led the field for most of the race, but as they neared the finish line, he turned his head to see where Bannister was. Landy lost step, which was all the Englishman needed to pull ahead and win. But the race was a victory for both runners, as for the first time in history two runners in the same race completed the mile in under four minutes — Bannister posting a winning 3.58.8, and Landy right behind at 3.59.6.

17. What was the Brill Bend?

A. The Brill Bend was a revolutionary new reverse jumping style that really caught on with competitive high jumpers. Its inventor was Debbie Brill, a young woman from Mission, B.C., who in 1971 became the first North American woman to clear 6'0", and in 1982, just a few months after giving birth to her child, set a world indoor record with a 1.99-metre jump. Brill won gold medals at the 1970 Canada Games and 1971 Pan-American Games. This talented athlete holds the world record for the women's over-35 mark — 1.89 metres — and still makes her home in British Columbia.

18. Which Canadian held co-ownership of two world records in track — the 100-yard dash and the 100-metre?

A. Harry Jerome was born in Prince Albert, Saskatchewan, and moved to Vancouver when he was 12. A natural athlete, he began breaking records when still a teenager. Jerome received a scholarship to attend the University of Oregon, where he was able to achieve a higher education while at the same time benefitting from the school's excellent track program. In 1959, in Saskatoon, he tied the world record by running the 100-metres in ten seconds flat — a record that would stand for almost a decade. Soon after, however, he began to be plagued by injury problems and it wouldn't be until the mid-60s before he hit his stride again, winning the bronze medal in the 100-metres at the 1964 Tokyo Olympics. Following his retirement in 1968, Jerome became an activist for social equality and for greater funding for amateur sport. Jerome passed away in 1982 at the young age of 42. Every year an award in his name is given out to an outstanding leader in the Canadian black community.

19. What Quebec television host is also a multi-record breaking athlete?

A. Chantal Petitclerc never really showed much of an interest in sports, so it was a surprise to all when, after a serious accident left her a paraplegic, a fourteen-year-old Chantal developed a great interest in competitive athletics. Debuting in her first wheelchair race in 1991, she has been dominant in race events ever since, setting several records over the course of her career , and winning five medals (two gold) at the 1996 Atlanta Paralympics. She has also been the television host for the Lotto Quebec draws and a show called "Pareil pas Pareil." A busy supporter for several charities, Chantal's dream is to see wheelchair racing recognized at the Olympic Games.

20. What Canadian won gold in the triathlon at the 2000 Sydney Olympics?

A. On September 16, 2000, Simon Whitfield a native of Kingston, Ontario, now based in B.C., joined a group of elite athletes to compete in the Olympic debut of what many consider the hardest event in all sports: the triathlon. Ranked 21st in the world, Simon was thought to be a longshot to place in the medals in this tough field, and early on he didn't appear to be proving any doubters wrong: at the end of the swimming leg of the race, Simon was well back of the lead in 22nd place. But then in the cycling portion, he moved up dramatically to 12th, and in the final stage — the 10k run — he bolted past the opposition to win the gold medal and the title of the world's greatest triathlete.

21. What was Canadian Ronald McDonald's sporting triumph?

A. Now, since the accomplishment occurred at the 1898 Boston Marathon, you can bet it wasn't the current fast food spokesman that we're talking about. This fleet-footed namesake originally hailed from Antigonish, Nova Scotia, but left Canada to attend school in the New England area. In fact, he was a student at Boston College that April day over a century ago when he was victorious in the second running of this famous marathon. Though McDonald was listed as an American in many of the Boston newspapers' reports, he was born in Canada and returned here to live later in his life.

22. Was there ever a controversy over an early Boston Marathon result involving a Canadian?

A. In 1901, returning champion Jack Caffery of Hamilton, Ontario — the favourite going into the prestigious 26.2-mile race — was going head to head with fellow Canadian and 1898 champion Ronald McDonald. The race was one that always generated a lot of interest, but in this year there was a great deal of interest from the gambling industry, and a large amount of money had been bet on the outcome. With Caffery solidly out in the lead with the race well into its second half, someone handed McDonald a wet sponge. Soon after he used it, he started to slow, and then stopped running entirely and was whisked away by concerned friends. McDonald's physician, Dr. J.S. Thompson, claimed that he detected traces of chloroform in his patient's sponge. McDonald's trainer, John W. Bowler, on the other hand, said that it was the athlete's doctor who gave him some pills that were supposed to stimulate him but had the opposite effect. The truth never did come out and the controversy remained to be argued over for many years to come.

23. What sport did Bruce Kidd excel in?

A. Bruce Kidd of Toronto was only 17 years old when he first burst onto the international track and field scene by winning an indoor two-mile race in Boston in 1961. To make this win even more spectacular he did it in record time, breaking the U.S. record for the race. Not a bad feat for this unknown schoolboy from Canada. Kidd would win a number of high profile races in his career, but his greatest victory was in 1962 when he won the gold medal in the six-mile race at the British Empire Games in Perth, Australia. Among the honours Kidd received before his career was cut short due to chronic injuries were the 1961 Lou Marsh Trophy and Canada's Outstanding Athlete Award in 1962 and 1963. Kidd has become a notable author and a very vocal and respected sports and social critic.

WATER SPORTS

1. What was Alexandre Despatie's big claim to Canadian sports fame?

A. The amazing Alexandre made us all proud when at the 1998 Commonwealth Games in Malaysia he won a gold medal in platform diving. That accomplishment made him the youngest male ever to win an international diving event at the tender age of 15. Born in Laval, Quebec, he was named as the Canadian Junior Male Athlete of the Year in 1998–99.

2. Who was the first person to complete a non-stop double crossing of the English Channel?

A. Cindy Nicholas is another one of those people who instantly attracts others with her intelligence and down-to-earth humour. Along with her accomplishments in multiple record-breaking swims of Lake Ontario, she is affectionately known in

Great Britain as the Queen of the Channel. On September 7, 1977, she became the first female accomplish the feat of a non-stop double-crossing of the famed English Channel.

After her swimming career, Cindy graduated from law school and entered the political arena as an MP. She now tends to her successful law practice and her family, but has told me that when time allows she still swims laps in her pool.

3. How many Olympic gold medals have Kathleen Heddle and Marnie McBean won in their magnificent rowing careers?

A. These two amazing athletes won their first two gold medals at the 1992 Barcelona Olympics, one win coming in pairs rowing and the other as part of the Canadian eights crew. Four years later in Atlanta, the duo won gold in the double sculls event to bring their total to three career Olympic golds.

Marilyn Bell

4. Who was the first person to swim across Lake Ontario?

A. Marilyn Bell was a sixteen-year-old high schooler when, on September 9, 1954, she outlasted the legendary Florence Chadwick in a head-to-head battle to become the first to conquer the 32-mile wide lake. Marilyn's accomplishments captured the imaginations of all Canadians, and her lake crossing made this humble Toronto-born schoolgirl the most famous athlete in Canada at the time.

5. What was the most famous Canadian sailing vessel ever built?

The Bluenose

A. The 143-foot, 285-tonne *Bluenose* was launched on March 26, 1921, and proved herself not only to be an able fishing vessel, but also the unbeatable victor in scores of international races. She was fondly nicknamed "Stormalong" or "Old Weatherleg" by the many admirers of this Nova Scotian jewel, and was one of the proudest symbols of Maritime spirit. But alas, with racing challenges dwindling and the fishing industry on the east coast slowing down, the *Bluenose* was sold to a trading company and used as a freight carrier. She met her demise on a Haitian reef in 1946.

6. What did George Brown of Herring Cove, Nova Scotia, accomplish?

A. There's a monument in Herring Cove to this gentleman, who was a world renowned champion in the sport of rowing. As an amateur, Brown won literally dozens of competitions and placed second to reigning world professional champ Joseph Sadler of the U.S. at the 1871 Halifax Aquatic Carnival. At that point he turned pro and over the next few years beat all comers who challenged his rowing supremacy. But Brown could not forget the one man who had beaten him, and repeatedly attempted to persuade Sadler to meet him in a rematch. After a couple of years of on-again off-again negotiations, Sadler finally agreed to the race, but in 1875, Brown suffered a fatal stroke while training for the matchup. His funeral in Halifax was one of the largest ever and all the provincial flags flew at half mast.

7. Who was Levi Rogers and what was his claim to Canadian sports fame?

A. "Shorty" Rogers was one of the most famous athletes ever to come out of Newfoundland. The absolute King in the rowing world, his name became synonymous with the respected and historic Newfoundland Regatta. His knowledge and skill made him one of the most sought after coxswains and coaches in the country. Rogers competed for an amazing 58 years and coxed his crews to over 300 wins. A tireless competitor, he won his last race in 1962 at the age of 75.

8. What is the oldest known sporting event in Canada?

A. Until 1949, the Queen's Plate was the oldest annual event in the country, but when Newfoundland entered Confederation, it brought with it an event that was even older: the Newfoundland Regatta. The Regatta is over 185 years old and still going strong. We have proof of its age in the August 6, 1816 Newfoundland papers *The Gazette* and *The Advertizer*, which both had articles calling for people to attend the boat race the following Monday. By the end of the nineteenth century, the Regatta had grown to such a status that employers often granted their staff time off to attend the event. The Regatta was famous for its all-comers regulations, and there was a women's division set up back as far as 1855.

9. Who was the first Canadian woman to swim the English Channel?

A. It was in 1951 that a twenty-five-year-old wife and mother of three by the name of Winnie Roach Leuszler took up the challenge. Leuszler swam the width of the channel from Calais to Dover in an incredible time of 13 hours and 25 minutes — only a couple of minutes slower than the standing record at the time. Leuszler was also a footnote to another great marathon swimming story: she was the third woman when Marilyn Bell outlasted Florence Chadwick and conquered Lake Ontario in September 1954.

10. Which Canadian athlete had to wait over a year to be presented with her Olympic gold medal?

A. Synchronized swimming champion Sylvie Frechette from Quebec went into the 1992 Olympic Games in Barcelona fresh from the tragedy of her fiancé's suicide the week before the opening of the Games. Frechette showed courage and strength in giving what should have been a gold medal performance. But a judging error was committed by the Brazilian judge, who punched the wrong score into the computer, and through that mistake Frechette was knocked down to the silver medal position. Even with the Canadian reps and the Brazilian judge pleading for the miscarriage to be reversed, the Olympic committee incredibly refused to overturn the original decision and awarded American Krysten Babb the gold medal. It was only after lengthy appeals and arguments from Canadian officials that on December 15, 1993 — over a year after the actual competition — the gold was finally placed around the neck of the true Olympic champion in a special ceremony at the Montreal Forum.

11. How many medals did Silken Laumann win in her Olympic endeavours?

A. Silken Laumann's career included many stellar moments, but none so memorable as her courageous performance in

the 1992 Olympics in Barcelona. By the time 1992 came along she was already the world single sculls champion and had won a bronze medal with her sister Daniele in the double sculls at the 1984 Olympics. A couple of months before the 1992 Games Silken's boat was rammed by another boat in training, resulting in a broken ankle

Silken Laumann

and ligament damage. Doctors offered little hope that Silken would be able to compete in the Games. But she made a remarkable recovery, and not only competed in the Olympics, but won a bronze medal. Four years later Silken added to her medal count a silver medal in the 1996 Atlanta Games, bringing her total to three Olympic medals. She was awarded the Lou Marsh Trophy in 1991, and was the Canadian Press Female Athlete of the Year in 1991 and 1992.

Ned Hanlan

12. Who was Canada's first official athletic world champion?

A. It was the talented, sometimes controversial Edward "Ned" Hanlan, who won the title in November 1880 in the sport of single sculls rowing. It was reported that over 100,000 people attended the race in London, England, as Hanlan defeated Edward Trickett along the Thames River. He successfully defended his world title six times before losing it to Australian William Beach in 1884.

A colourful and flamboyant athlete, Hanlan would please the crowds by stopping mid-race to chat with or blow kisses at spectators. After his retirement, he took up coaching at the university level, ran his family hotel on Toronto Island, and served for a time as a city alderman. In 1926, Toronto erected a large statue to Hanlan on the Canadian National Exhibition grounds.

13. Rodney Harback had some luck on Great Bear Lake in the Northwest Territories. What exactly happened to him?

A. With the thousands of beautiful lakes in Canada you can bet that there's a million or two fishing tales to go along with them. Well according to the 2000 edition of *The Guinness Book of World Records*, Mr. Harback's story is definitely no big-one-that-got-away story. It seems that on January 19, 1991, he reeled in a 66 pound, 8 ounce lake trout — which, according to the Guinness people, is the heaviest fish of its kind ever caught.

14. What Canadian female athlete accomplished the feat of swimming across all the Great Lakes?

A. In September 1988, Vickie Keith began this huge under-taking. By the end of the month she had completed her quest by successfully conquering each of the Great Lakes. She swam a total of 165 miles, spending 160.5 hours in the water. A selfless person, Keith has raised literally hundreds of thousands of dollars in these swims — all of which has been directed to several charities, especially those that benefit the disabled. This star of the lakes has also devoted herself to working with children and in recent years has taken to writing children's books.

15. Who was the first Canadian woman to win two gold medals at one Olympics?

A. Born in Beaconsfield, Quebec, in 1964, synchronized swim-mer Carolyn Waldo took up water sports at the age of 10, to the surprise of those around her: she had been terrified of water ever since nearly drowning at the age of 3. Moving to Calgary in the early 80s to train with the well-known synchronized swimming coach Debbie Muir, it didn't take long for Waldo to start making a name for herself, and at the 1984 Los Angeles Olympics she won a silver medal in the solo swim. Four years later in Seoul, Waldo won the gold in the same event, and then captured another gold in the pairs competition with her partner, Michelle Cameron.

16. Who was Miss Supertest III?

A. The fastest speedboat of her time, Miss Supertest III was owned by Canadian James Thompson and on November 1, 1957, set a world record by travelling a blistering 184.54 mph at Picton, Ontario. The boat, piloted by native Ontarian Bob Hayward, took on and beat all challengers, and won the prestigious Harmsworth Trophy — the top award in speedboat racing — in 1959, 1960, and 1961. These wins broke a thirty-year domination of the sport by the Americans. Tragically, Bob Hayward was killed on September 10, 1961, racing Miss Supertest II, the sister boat and test ship for the champ. Miss Supertest III was retired soon after.

17. What two firsts did Sylvie Bernier accomplish at the 1984 Los Angeles Olympics?

A. This champion diver was responsible for two Olympic firsts: she was the first Canadian diver ever to win a gold medal, and she was the first Quebec woman in any sport to win Olympic gold.

Bernier began her career at the age of 10, and was a member of the Canadian national team at the age of 14. Winning a silver medal at the 1982 Commonwealth Games and bronze at both the 1983 World University and Pan-Am Games, she was considered one of the favourites going into the 1984 Los Angeles Olympics. Once there, she didn't disappoint, winning the gold medal in the 3-metre springboard and setting a new Olympic record of 530.70 points.

18. What do you get when you mix a Canadian champion diver with an accomplished Canadian synchronized swimmer?

A. It's a riddle that has its answer in the lives of British Columbia's famed Athans family. George Athans Sr. won a gold medal in the 1950 British Empire Games, while his wife, Irene Hartzell, was a nationally ranked swimmer and four-time Manitoba synchronized swimming champion. And the accomplishments of these two have been surpassed by those of their offspring. George Sr. and Irene produced a family that has excelled in the sports of skiing — both snow and water. The best known of the clan would be Canadian Hall of Famer George Athans Jr., who along with having many Canadian titles to his credit was one of the most dominant water skiers of his era with a total of three world titles and numerous world records to his credit. His younger brother Greg, meanwhile, was the first Canadian athlete to win a gold medal at the Canada Games in both the alpine slalom and water-skiing tricks categories. Greg was also the world pro freestyle alpine champion in 1976 and world mogul champ in 1980. Add to the equation brother Gary, a great success himself in both alpine and water skiing, and you have the core of one of the greatest sports dynasties in Canadian history.

19. What Olympic gold medalist's life was cut short at the age of 25 by a hit-and-run driver?

A. Victor Davis of Guelph, Ontario, was one of those driven athletes whose desire to win every race entered was second to none. After much international success, Davis proved himself to be the best in the world when, at the age of 20, he took home three medals from the 1984 Los Angeles Olympics. Victor won gold in the 200-metre breaststroke, and then followed it up with silver medals in the 100-metre breaststroke and the 4x100 medley relay. On November 13, 1989, Davis was killed in a hit-and-run accident in Montreal. He won't easily be forgotten.

Victor Davis, 1984 Olympic gold medalist

20. Who won the first Olympic swimming gold medal for Canada?

A. Brought up in Montreal, the young George Hodgson took like the proverbial fish to water and by his late teens was taking part in international swimming tournaments. In 1911 in a prestigious sporting event put together in London, England, to help celebrate King George V coronation, Hodgson won a one mile race against some of the best competition in the world, despite never having swam the distance before. But Hodgson's best-known accomplishments came at the Stockholm Olympics when the Canadian won gold in the 400 and 1500-metre freestyle, setting world records in both that would stand for a dozen years until broken at the 1924 Olympics by Johnny Weissmuller. After Hodgson's two golds Canada would not produce another gold medal swimmer for more than 50 years.

21. Which Canadian Olympic swimming hero won 3 medals at the Games, one of each colour?

A. At the 1988 Seoul Games Calgary-born Mark Tewksbury swam the lead breast stroke leg for Canada's silver medal 4x100-metre relay team, and at the 1992 Barcelona Olympics he struck for two more medals — bronze in the 4x100-metre relay and gold in the 100-metre back stroke. Setting over half a dozen world records throughout his career, Mark has been in great demand as a public speaker since his retirement, and is actively involved in many sporting and humanitarian endeavours.

22. Who was the first Canadian woman to ever win an Olympic gold medal in swimming?

A. Whitby, Ontario's Anne Ottenbrite was the talented lady who accomplished this feat at the 1984 Los Angeles Games by winning not only the gold in the 200-metre breast stroke but also a silver and a bronze in the 100-metre breast stroke and the 4x100-metre relay respectively. Ottenbrite herself almost didn't get the opportunity to compete at the Games: a knee injury had kept her from competing at the Olympic trials. But Canadian officials had faith in this young lady's talents and allowed her to compete in Los Angeles — with golden results.

23. What were the team of George Hungerford and Roger Jackson famous for?

A. Hungerford and Jackson, or the "Golden Rejects" as they were called, won the gold medal in rowing at the 1964 Tokyo Olympics. Hungerford was a member of the eight-man crew until a bout with mononucleosis had him dropped from the team. The Vancouver native, after somewhat recovering from the illness, started training with the Torontonian Jackson, who had lost his pairs partner when he was moved up to the eights crew to take Hungerford's place. By the time the two made it over to Tokyo, they were really clicking together, but nobody gave this brand new team much of a chance of beating the strong German or Dutch teams. To everyone's surprise, they did just that, edging out the second place Dutch team by half a length and winning Canada its first Summer Olympic gold medal since 1956.

24. What sport is world champion Adam Purdy so dominant in?

A. Purdy, a native of London, Ontario, is the world record holder in the Paralympic 100-metre backstroke. As a member of the London Aquatic Club he first made the national team in 1994, and at the 1996 Summer Paralympic Games he finished fourth in the backstroke. Disappointed, his resolve grew even larger and it was at the 1998 world championships that he won the 100-metre backstroke event in world record time, swam on the gold-medal winning 4x100 medley relay team, and took silver in the 200. But it was at the 2000 Sydney Games that this talented young man won a gold medal in his forte race — the backstroke — breaking his own world record time en route.

25. What Canadian athlete posed au natural in *Time* magazine?

A. Just before the 2000 Sydney Olympics, Waneek Horn-Miller decided to pose nude, holding only a strategically placed water polo ball, for the Canadian edition of *Time*. She believes that the artistic photograph and the publicity it has garnered helped raise the sport's profile. The Native Canadian co-captained the water polo squad to a fifth-place finish at the Olympic Games. Horn-Miller has also won 20 gold medals at the Indigenous Games and was elected a record three times as athlete of the year at Carleton University, where she graduated with a degree in political science. In spite of her sporting accomplishments, Horn-Miller may be best remembered for the national coverage she received at the age of 14 when, during the Oka crisis, she was wounded in the chest by a soldier's bayonet.

26. What courageous Canadian athlete overcame a bout with cancer to win a medal at the 2000 Sydney Olympics?

A. Winnipeg's Emma Robinson was one of the mainstays of the Canadian rowing team, having been part of the silver medal eights team at the 1996 Atlanta Games and the world championship pairs team, with partner Alison Korn, in 1997. Early in 1999, Robinson was diagnosed with thyroid cancer, and in March of that year underwent surgery to remove the stricken gland. Where most would have given up, this incredible athlete's resolve only heightened, and within months she and her new partner Theresa Luke won the World Cup Regatta and then a gold medal at the Pan-Am Games. At the 2000 Sydney Games, again competing in the eights event, Robinson again visited the medal podium after she and her teammates placed third in the final.

27. What heroic adventure occurred to Canadian yachtsman Larry Lemieux at the 1988 Seoul Olympics?

A. Edmonton native Larry Lemieux, one of the finest Finn class sailors in the world, was in a comfortable second place during the final race to determine gold when he came upon injured sailors from Singapore whose ship had just sunk. Instinctively, he forgot about the race and rushed to rescue the drowning men. Although this selfless, heroic act cost him an Olympic medal, Lemieux was awarded a special Olympic Sportsmanship Award and has gone down in Canadian and Olympic history as a true hero of the Games.

28. Who is regarded as the founder of the sport of synchronized swimming?

A. Montreal-born Margaret "Peg" Seller was quite an athlete in her own rite, excelling as a swimmer, diver, and water polo player when she led a group of women in the 1920s in developing a new form of water sport called synchronized swimming. The style of swimming was popularized in the cinema by such Esther Williams films as *Bathing Beauty* and *Million Dollar Mermaid*. As synchronized swimming began to gain acceptance at international meets, Peg Seller kept up a persistent lobby to have the sport recognized as an Olympic event, and in 1984 her efforts were rewarded. Since that time, Canadian's have been one of the powerhouses of the sport with such athletes as Carolyn Waldo, Sylvie Frechette, and Peggy and Vicky Vilagos among those winning Olympic medals.

29. Did Alex Baumann ever win an Olympic gold medal in swimming?

A. Alex Baumann's greatest success came at the 1984 Olympics in Los Angeles. Baumann won gold medals in both the 400 and 200-metre individual medleys, setting new world records in each event. Baumann, who moved to Canada from Czechoslovakia at the age of 5, was one of the most dominant swimmers of his era, establishing 32 national and six world records.

Alex Baumann,
double gold medal winner,
1984 Olympics

30. Which Canadian female dominated the swimming pool at the 2000 Paralympics?

A. It was eighteen-year-old Calgary native Jessica Sloan who came away with an impressive six gold medals at the Games. A member of the University of Calgary Swim Club, Sloan tore up the pool, striking gold in the 50 and 100-metre freestyle, the 100-metre breaststroke, the 200-metre individual medley, and both the medley and freestyle relays. With a large chunk of her career still to come, you can be sure that we'll be hearing of many more triumphs from this extraordinary young athlete.

WINTER SPORTS

1. Over the past forty years, what sport has Canada almost single-handedly dominated in both men's and women's divisions?

A. Since 1959, Canada has had a stranglehold on the sport of curling winning more than 25 world championships. And, on the women's side, since 1980, we've won ten world titles.

2. Who was the first Canadian to win the men's downhill skiing World Cup?

A. On March 5, 1982, Steve Podborski became not only the first Canadian, but the first non-European to win the downhill award. It was the first of many titles to be won by one of the charter members of the club known as The Crazy Canucks. Podborski turned to commentating after retiring, and is an active ambassador for the sport worldwide.

Nancy Greene

3. What Canadian female won both a gold and silver medal at the 1968 Grenoble Olympics?

A. Rossland, B.C. native Nancy Greene burst onto the international ski scene in the mid-60s, and in 1968 she capped her amazing career with the two medals in the giant slalom. After her retirement, she became coach of our national team, and to this day remains one of the finest ambassadors of the sport that Canada has ever developed.

4. Why was Charles Gorman known as North America's fastest man?

A. Gorman, a native of St. John, New Brunswick, was probably the most dominant speedskater of his time, winning titles and setting world records that would not be broken for more than 20 years. He won his first world title in 1926, and in the following months took home gold in several important tournaments. The year 1927 turned out to be the year in which he would completely dominate the sport when he won the Canadian, U.S., and world championships, breaking world records in the one-sixth mile and 440-yard events. Unfortunately, at the 1928 St. Moritz Olympics Gorman, who was the favourite in the 500-metre race, was slowed down when a competitor stumbled in front of him causing the Canadian to finish a disappointing seventh.

5. Did Anne Heggtveit ever win a medal for Canada at the Olympics? If so, what sport did she win it in?

A. If ever a girl was meant to be a world class skier, it was Ottawa-born Anne Heggtveit, whose family boasted accomplished skiers on both her parents' sides of the family. Her dad and uncle were both Canadian cross-country champs, and her uncle on her mom's side was a member of the Canadian team at

Anne Heggtveit

the 1932 and 1936 Olympics. Anne herself got an early start in the sport, racing competitively by the age of 7. At 15, she became the youngest person to win the giant slalom World Cup race at Holmen Kollen, Norway. But the best to come was at the 1960 Winter Olympics at Squaw Valley, where she won the gold medal for Canada in the slalom, finishing over three seconds faster than the second place competitor.

6. Who won a gold medal in the giant slalom at the 1976 Innsbruck Olympics?

A. Eighteen-year-old Timmins, Ontario native Kathy Kreiner accomplished this championship deed. Kathy came from a skiing family: her father had been the long-time national ski team doctor, and her older sister Laurie was a member of the national ski team. She wasn't given much of a chance to win the event, what with the great world champion Rosi Mittermaier expected to sweep the slalom, downhill, and giant slalom. But in true champion-style, Kreiner pulled off the upset and copped the gold.

7. How many medals did Myriam Bedard win for Canada in the Olympics biathlon?

A. Bedard of Loretteville, Quebec, received a great deal of shooting training as an army cadet in her teens and picked up tremendous skiing skills to finish the athletic equation. After steadily moving up the world rankings, she won a bronze medal in the 15-kilometre event at the Albertville Olympics. After winning the 1993 world titles, she was the frontrunner for Olympic gold in 1994. And Bedard came through, winning gold in both the 7.5 and 15-kilometre events at the Lillehammer Games, bringing her career Olympic medal total to three.

8. Who won Canada's gold medal in women's Olympic curling at the 1998 Nagano Games?

A. Sandra Schmirler of Biggar, Saskatchewan, will go down in Canadian sports history as one of the most talented and endearing athletes to ever represent our country. Her death in March 2000 at the young age of 36 stunned a nation that over the course of a decade had taken this world champion curler into their hearts. A champion athlete, who won three Canadian championships (1993, 1994, and 1997) and three world titles (also in 1993, 1994, and 1997), she was the odds on favourite to win gold at the 1998 Nagano Olympics. Schmirler didn't disappoint, defeating the Danish rink 7–5 in the gold medal match.

9. How old is the Royal Montreal Curling Club?

A. The Royal Montreal Curling Club is the oldest sports organization in Canada, dating back two centuries. The club got its start when a group of 20 immigrants from curling's home, Scotland, met at Gillis Coffee House on January 22, 1807, to set down the rules of the club. Thirty years later, the club would make history by building the first indoor rink in Canada.

10. Which former speedskating Olympic champion is the pride and joy of St. Hubert, Quebec?

A. Gaeton Boucher was one of the most dominant speedskaters on the world scene throughout the late 1970s and 1980s. He made his first mark on the Olympic stage at the 1980 Lake Placid Olympics when he took the silver medal in the 1000-metre race. Then four years later at the Sarajevo Olympics, he captured gold in both the 1,000 and 1,500-metre races, and a bronze in the 500-metre sprint.

11. Which province has won the most Briers?

A. The Brier is the top curling tournament in Canada. Between the first Brier in 1927 and the most recent in 2001, Manitoba has won the event the most often, having taken the tournament 26 times. Alberta is second with 18 wins, and Ontario is third with 8. New Brunswick, Prince Edward Island, and the Yukon/Northwest Territories have yet to win the annual classic.

12. Who were the Richardson Rink?

A. Saskatchewan has always been curling country, so it was shocking to all that lived and breathed the sport that by the time the 1959 tournament rolled around, Saskatchewan had won only one previous Brier championship. But that would soon change with the explosion onto the curling scene of the Richardson Rink. Brothers Ernie and Garnet Richardson, along with their cousins Wes and Arnold Richardson, not only won that Brier in 1959, but went on to win three more, in 1960, 1962, and 1963. On the international stage, the Richardsons captured four world championships, in 1959, 1960, 1962, and 1963. This young team popularized a new, wide-open style of play and added new blood to the sport, raising curling's profile around the country.

13. Which Canadian was the first athlete to ever win an Olympic gold medal in the sport of snowboarding?

A. Ross Rebagliati became the first ever gold medal winner in the young sport of snowboarding on February 8, 1998, at the Nagano Olympics. What this event is best remembered for, however, is the events that unfolded afterwards. On February 11, after a drug test showed traces of THC (the major intoxicant of marijuana) the International Olympic Committee decided to strip the young Canadian of his medal. Rebagliati and the Canadian contingent immediately launched an appeal, claiming that marijuana does not enhance performance, and an international arbitration board agreed. The IOC's decision was reversed, and Ross was again a gold medallist. This brouhaha earned Rebagliati a short-lived period of fame, even landing him guest shots on American talk shows like *The Late Show with David Letterman*.

14. What Canadian downhill skier won the world championships in 1970 at the age of 16?

A. Betsy Clifford of Ottawa packed a lot of success into her relatively short career: at 14 she was the youngest competitor at the 1968 Olympics; two years later she became the youngest athlete ever to win the world championship in the grand slalom; and a year later she finished second in the slalom category. By the time she retired in 1976 at the age of 23, Clifford had finished in the top ten at the world championships more than a dozen times.

15. Who is generally regarded worldwide as the fastest woman on skates?

A. Catriona Le May Doan, the 1998 Canadian female athlete of the year, has been the most dominant female speedskater in the world over the past five years. This Saskatoon native is a natural sprinter, and has been crowned world champion four times in the 500-metre division. At the 1998 Nagano Olympics, Catriona captured the gold in the 500-metre event and bronze in the 1,000-metre race. She is the only woman to ever break the 38 second barrier in the 500-metres.

Lela Brooks, first Canadian woman to win a gold medal in speedskating in the 1926 world championships.

16. Who was the first Canadian woman to be acknowledged as an official world champion?

A. By the time Toronto's Lela Brooks was 18 years old, she had already won many national and regional championships. In 1926 she broke through internationally, winning the world speedskating championship, the first Canadian woman to hold a world championship in any sport.

17. Who were the Crazy Canucks?

A. It struck many people as strange that a country that had produced so many successful women skiers was unable to produce a competitive men's team. Until, that is, a group of young Canadians with a devil-may-care attitude burst onto the ski scene in the mid-70s. Ken Read, Steve Podborski, Dave Irwin, and Dave Murray captured the imaginations of not just Canada, but the entire ski world and became what many consider to be the greatest ski team ever. Nicknamed the Crazy Canucks, they won a collective 14 World Cup races, highlighted by Podborski's World Cup championship in 1982. The Canucks reigned near the top of the standings for over a decade before they all retired from competition to pursue other interests. Unfortunately, team member Dave Murray died in 1990 after a courageous battle with cancer.

The Crazy Canucks

18. Who are the only two Canadian men to have won Olympic medals in downhill skiing?

A. Canadians have had great success in women's Olympic skiing with such gold-medal stars of the slopes as Anne Heggtveit, Nancy Greene, and Karen Lee-Gartner, but only two Canadian men have ever medalled at the Games, each time taking the bronze: Steve Podborski in 1980, and Edi Pdivinsky in 1994.

19. What Canadian male has been a major force in international speedskating over the past decade?

A. Born in 1976, in Humboldt, Saskatchewan, and now based in Red Deer, Alberta, Jeremy Wotherspoon began skating at the age of eight, and by the time he hit his teens he was considered one of the finest up-and-coming talents in the world of speedskating. He has won many accolades and titles since his junior days, and is now generally regarded as the number one skater in the sport. Along with an Olympic silver medal at the 1998 Nagano Games, he has won four World Cup crowns in the 1,000-meter race and has been king in both the 1,000 and 500-metre sprints in 1998, 1999, and 2000.

20. What speedskater picked up silver medals in the 500-metre sprint at both the 1994 and 1998 Olympics?

A. Selected in 1996 as Canada's outstanding female athlete, Winnipeg-born and Calgary-based Susan Auch started speedskating at the age of 12. In 1988, she made her first appearance on the Olympic podium as a member of the bronze-medal team in the relays, at the time only a demonstration sport. Six years later in Lillehammer, she won the silver medal in the 500-metre, then repeated her success in 1998 at Nagano. Auch then announced her retirement from skating. But the retirement was short-lived, and Auch returned to the rink. A great all-around athlete, she also made an unsuccessful try at the national cycling team in 2000 when she placed fourth in qualifying.

21. Who is the only dog sled racer in the Canadian Sports Hall of Fame?

A. The sport of dog racing, like those of canoeing, shooting, and skiing, developed out of the harsh realities of northern living. Canadian Emile St. Godard became the premier dog racer of his time, winning most of the major tourneys held in Canada and the northern United States. His rivalry with American Leonard Seppalo drew widespread attention after it was learned that Seppalo had rushed a diphtheria serum in record time to the city of Nome to avert an outbreak of the dreaded disease. The two had faced each other many times over the years, with the Canadian coming out on top in the majority of races. St. Godard's biggest career victory came in 1932 when he won a gold medal at the Lake Placid Olympics, where dog sled racing appeared as a demonstration sport.

22. What Canadian athletes were affectionately nicknamed "The Intellectuals"?

A. At the 1964 Innsbruck Olympics, the "Intellectuals" were the gold medal victors in the bobsled competition. The nickname was in recognition of the elite scholastic backgrounds of the four men: Vic Emery had graduated from Harvard, Doug Anakin from Queen's, and Peter Kirby from McGill, while Vic's brother, John Emery, was a well respected plastic surgeon in Montreal. Their win was the only gold medal performance for Canada in the 1964 Games.

23. Who was the first Canadian to win the world junior ski jumping championships?

A. Ottawa, Ontario's own Horst Bulau was a born daredevil on the ski slopes, and by the age of 16 he had burst recorded wins in the Canadian championships and on the World Cup circuit. He was so dominant in the sport that through the 1983 and 1984 seasons alone Horst won a dozen medals in World Cup competitions.

Wrestling & the Martial Arts

1. Who tore off wrestling great Yukon Eric's ear, and where did this ghastly incident occur?

A. Back in the mid-1950s, Yukon Eric and Walter "Killer" Kowalski had quite a feud going in the ring (they were friends outside of it). One night at a show at the Montreal Forum, Kowalski came off the rope knee first and accidentally tore off a big chunk of Eric's ear. The two wrestlers and their promoters capitalized on the publicity that resulted from the incident, and turned the accident into a series of sold out shows around North America.

2. Who are the Canadian duo known as the "Twin Dragons"?

A. Identical twins Michael and Martin McNamara have been driving forces in the sport of kickboxing in Canada for over 25 years, training more than a dozen fighters to either North

American and world championships. Their latest protégé is the ISKA Women's Super flyweight world champ Chantal Nadon of North Bay, Ontario. Along with running their Twin Dragons Martial Arts Schools, the Dragons have written, produced, and starred in a number of action films.

Kickboxing's Twin Dragons

3. Who was the co-holder of the WWF tag team championship with Bret Hart?

A. The goateed powerhouse was Jim "The Anvil" Neidhart, who developed his wrestling skills under the tutelage of Bret's father, Stu Hart. Neidhart had already made a name for himself in professional sports prior to putting on the tights: before turning to professional wrestling, he was an integral part of the NFL Oakland Raiders' famous defensive line from the mid- to late 1970s.

4. What sport did Doug Rogers excel in?

A. Canada had never been a powerhouse in the Japanese sport of Judo, so it was a surprise when a big 260-pound Canadian by the name of Doug Rogers came along and won a silver medal at the 1964 Tokyo Olympics.

5. What pro wrestling world champion used to brag that he was "Canada's Greatest Athlete"?

A. Whether or not his claim was valid, no one would want to tangle with the wrecking machine from Alberta by the name of Gene Kiniski. Kiniski was a college wrestling and football star who was named the All-American team in both sports while at Arizona State. After graduation, he turned to professional wrestling, and on January 7, 1966, he defeated the legendary Lou Thez for the NWA world championship, which he held for almost three years.

6. Who founded and presided over the Alberta-based sports organization called Stampede Wrestling?

A. The Hart family name is synonymous with the sport of professional wrestling, not just in Canada but worldwide. Family patriarch Stu Hart founded his Stampede Wrestling in Calgary in 1948 and toured the company through the West. Stampede Wrestling became known as one of the premier training grounds for up-and-coming wrestlers, having produced the likes of such stars as Roddy Piper, Davey Boy Smith, and Stu's own sons (seven altogether, the most notable being Bret and the late Owen Hart).

7. What former world champion wrestler became one of this country's greatest spokespeople and fundraisers for children's charities?

A. William Potts, better known to his fans as Whipper Billy Watson, had a heart as big as himself, and he proved this by helping handicapped and underprivileged kids as a spokesman and fundraiser for children's charities. This terrific all-around athlete from Toronto won fame and fortune for twice winning the world championship — first in 1947 by pinning Bill Longson, and again in 1956 by defeating Lou Thez. This great humanitarian's career came to an end when he was hit by a car, crushing his legs. At the time of the accident he was delivering presents to a group of underprivileged children.

8. Which wrestling superstar grew up in the streets of Toronto before moving out west to learn his craft?

A. Roderick Toombs, better known as Rowdy Roddy Piper, was born in Scotland, but came to Canada as a wee lad and grew up in the rough Parkdale area of Toronto. Leaving home as a teenager, he made his way out west to learn the sport of professional wrestling, and became the youngest person ever to turn pro on the circuit at the age of 15. He lost his first match in 15 seconds to grizzled veteran Larry "The Axe" Hennig (father of Curt, better known as Mr. Perfect). But Piper was patient and improved quickly, and within a few years he was one of the largest draws in the business. Now retired from the mat wars, he has had a successful second career starring in a string of B action movies.

9. What Canadian sports family sported such colourful nicknames as "Mad Dog", "The Butcher", and "Luna"?

A. The Vachons of Montreal are among Quebec's many contributions to the world of professional wrestling. This colourful bunch created mayhem all over the world, and were among the biggest attractions on the wrestling circuit. Maurice, better known to fans and friends as "Mad Dog", got his start in the amateur version of the sport, and actually represented Canada as a middleweight wrestler at the 1948 Olympic Games. He and his brother Paul ("The Butcher") were tag team champions on several occasions, and Paul's daughter Angelle "Luna" Vachon, was a WWF mainstay throughout a good part of the 1990s.

10. Which Canadian pro wrestler's disputed win over world champion Lou Thez ended up splintering an entire major wrestling organization?

A. Edouard Weicz, better known to fans as Edouard Carpentier, originally came to Canada from France after World War II. Carpentier had been a hero in the French resistance, and was awarded the Croix de Guerre and the Croix des Combattants. Arriving in Canada, Edouard eventually took up the sport of professional wrestling, and on June 14, 1957, he defeated longtime National Wrestling Alliance (NWA) champion Lou Thez, only to have the NWA overturn the result, claiming that Carpentier had won on an illegal pinfall. The uproar that followed this decision led several NWA stars to leave and form the American Wrestling Association (AWA), which recognized Quebec's Carpentier as its heavyweight champion.

11. What Canadian-born NFL Hall of Famer was also a world champion wrestler?

A. Born in Canada in 1908, Bronko Nugurski was one of the all-time great fullbacks in the pre-modern era of football. He played college ball for Minnesota State and turned pro for the Chicago Bears in 1930. In his nine full seasons, this workhorse rushed for 4,031 yards. When he retired after the 1937 season (he would return for one more year in 1943), he took to wrestling full-time, and later that year he won the first of three world heavyweight wrestling championships. The highlight of his mat career came in 1939 when he defeated Lou Thez for the world's most prestigious title, the NWA championship.

12. What Canadian grappler was a U.S. college champion before turning his sights towards professional mat wars?

A. Earl McCready was a U.S. intercollegiate champion three times in his outstanding career at Oklahoma A&M. Born in Lansdowne, Ontario, and raised in Saskatchewan, this Canadian farm boy was over 6'0 tall and 200 pounds by the time he was 14. He began wrestling in high school, and won his first national title in 1926 at the age of 18. Then it was off to Oklahoma where he began his three-year dominance of amateur heavyweight wrestling wars. In 1930 at the British Empire Games he won a gold medal, and added to his incredible record for that year by winning every amateur wrestling title available in the U.S., Canada, and the British Commonwealth. With nothing more to accomplish in the amateur ranks, McCready turned pro, and remained one of the top contenders for the world title for most of his 25 years in the sport. His battles with Strangler Lewis, Jim Browning, Dick Shikat, and Jim Londos are considered to be classics. As a testament to his outstanding career, Earl McCready became the only Canadian to be elected to both the American and Canadian Sports Hall of Fame.

13. What connection does WWF superstar The Rock have with Canada?

A. Actually The Rock, aka Dwayne Johnson, has a couple of connections to our fair land, one personal and the other professional. The Rock's father, well known ex-star of the mat was Rocky "Soulman" Johnson, was actually born Wayde Bowles in Nova Scotia. While The Rock would one day follow in his father's footsteps as a grappler, he started out his athletic career as a football player, an in so doing made his other connection with Canada. After an outstanding college career with the University of Miami Hurricanes, Dwayne toiled with the Calgary Stampeders during the 1995 season. But after one season he wisely turned his eye towards a career in the world of sports entertainment.

14. Who won an Olympic gold medal in wrestling at the 2000 Sydney Olympics?

A. Daniel Igali was born in Nigeria, the eldest of seven children. This tough 151-pounder first came to Canada in 1994 as a member of Nigeria's Commonwealth Games team to compete in Victoria, B.C. Fearing political unrest in his own country, Igali defected here and by 1997 was able to compete in international competitions under Canada's banner. In 1999, Igali became the first Canadian to win the world championship in the 69-kilo category. But it was at the 2000 Sydney Games that this remarkable young man reached the pinnacle of his sport, winning the Olympic gold medal.

15. Who in Canadian sports was known as the "Iceman"?

A. The greatest kickboxing champ in Canadian history, Jean-Yves Theriault was nicknamed "Iceman" for his cool demeanour in the ring, his way of intimidating opponents with an icy stare. Born in 1955 in New Brunswick, Theriault won the Canadian middleweight kickboxing title in 1979, and his first world title followed in 1980. Theriault would go on to win 23 world championships in his distinguished career, and amassed an impressive record of 69 wins (61 of them by KO), 6 defeats, and 1 draw.

16. What wrestling star lost his life after falling from the rafters prior to a match?

A. Owen Hart was born in Calgary, the youngest boy in the huge family of wrestling legend Stu Hart and his wife. A successful wrestler with the WWF, the leading wrestling organization in the world, Owen was known for his high-flying ability and his in-ring feud with older brother Bret Hart. On May 23, 1999, while appearing on a pay-per-view show at the Kempler Arena in Kansas City, Hart was being lowered into the ring by cable when the body harness that held him malfunctioned and he fell to his death in front of the packed arena. Hart's family sued several parties for the tragic occurrence, eventually settling out of court for an undisclosed amount.

MISCELLANEOUS

1. What two brothers from Montreal have been the driving force behind the popularization of the sport of bodybuilding?

A. For more than half a century, Joe and Ben Weider have, through hard work and innovative marketing, taken the sport of bodybuilding from a lightly regarded pastime to a mainstream giant. Not ones to rest on their laurels, the Weiders, now well into their 70s, remain on the cutting edge of the sport in the 21st century.

2. Has a Canadian soccer team ever made it to the medal round at the Olympics?

A. As hard as it may seem to believe, not only have we made it to the medal round, but we actually won a gold medal when a team from Galt, Ontario, beat all comers in the St. Louis Games of 1904. Now, if we could just start doing that with our hockey teams!

3. Who shared the 1983 Canadian Athlete of the Year award with the Wayne Gretzky?

A. Well it doesn't get much better than the heroic Rick Hansen, who wheeled himself around the world to raise awareness for spinal cord research. Nothing against Wayne, for he truly is one of the greatest and classiest athletes that ever lived, but I think it's he who should have been honoured to share the award with Hansen.

4. What did the Canadian Olympic team do that was unusual during the opening ceremonies at the 1920 Games?

A. Almost unbelievably, we sent our whole contingent to Antwerp to proudly represent us, but when the opening ceremonies began there was no Canadian flag to be found. Our Canadian team had no choice but to march into the stadium carrying an empty flag pole.

5. Who has the fastest serve in tennis?

A. According to the *Guinness Book of World Records*, ex-Canadian (now playing for Britain) Greg Rusedski served a ball that was recorded at 149 mph at a Champions Cup Tournament in California in 1998.

6. Who was voted the top Canadian athlete of the first half of the 20th century?

A. Lionel Conacher was probably the most amazing all-around athlete ever produced in Canada — or anywhere else for that matter. To list all of his accomplishments would take half a book, so here are just some of his most notable:

- Ontario Wrestling Champion in 1916.
- In 1920, in his first official boxing match, won the Canadian Light-Heavyweight championship.
- Played baseball for the International Toronto Maple Leafs.
- Won championships in lacrosse with the Toronto Maitlands.
- Played football and won the Grey Cup in 1922 when the Argos beat the Edmonton Eskimoes 23–0, a game in which Conacher himself scored 15 points.
- Had a solid career in the National Hockey League for over a decade.
- Was a provincial and then federal politician who built himself as a champion for the poor.

This Canadian hero passed away playing in a softball game in 1954. I doubt we'll ever see another quite like him.

Lionel
Conacher

7. Which Canadian snooker player was the first player to ever shoot a perfect game in a world championship?

A. Over the past 20 years the game of snooker has grown into one of the country's most popular pastimes, and has moved from the seedy local poolroom (my first choice, let it be known) to upscale emporiums that cater to the Hoi Poloy of the felt-table set. Now much of this growth in Canada can be attributed to the success of Cliff Thorburn, who in the late 1970s and early 1980s was the first non-Brit to win a world championship. In 1980, he did what some thought was impossible, scoring a perfect game in the world championship final.

8. What did Canadian Yvon du Hamel do faster than anyone else?

A. In March 1973, he took his 900cc Kawasaki to the two and a quarter mile track at Daytona International Speedway and set a new world record for speed over a lap by completing the circuit in 56.149 seconds, hitting a top speed of 160.288 mph.

9. What former *Toronto Star* reporter wrote a classic treatise on bullfighting?

A. Nobel Prize-winning novelist Ernest Hemingway, who became almost as famous for his sporting endeavours as he did for his writing, worked as a reporter for *The Toronto Star* from 1920 to 1924, and lived in the city for part of that time. In 1932, he published *Death in the Afternoon*, a study of bullfighting in Spain that is regarded by many as the most accomplished English text on the sport.

10. Thomas Ryan invented one of Canada's most popular pastimes, a sport that many of us didn't even know was purely Canadian. What is this popular sport?

A. Thomas Ryan was a businessman who was in the bowling alley business in Toronto when he invented the game of five-pin bowling. It truly has become one of the most popular sports anywhere, as anyone who has had to wait for a lane to open up can attest to.

11. What was it that Alberta-born Ray Mitchell accomplished in November 1972?

A. Mitchell won the World Bowling championships in Hamburg, Germany, defeating bowlers from 38 different countries. Amazingly, Mitchell came late to his sport, not taking up bowling until 1961 when he was 30.

12. The world of professional sport owes a huge debt of gratitude to a real gentleman by the name of Athol Murray. What did this amazing man accomplish here in Canada?

A. This sports-minded Catholic priest, who was affectionately known as Père, founded Notre Dame College in Wilcox, Saskatchewan, which has developed some of the premier athletes in our country. Some notable Notre Dame graduates include Wendel Clark and Russ Courtnall.

13. Which former Canadian Athlete of the Year also worked as a penalty box official for the Los Angeles Kings?

A. Jockey Sandy Hawley has won almost every honour available in his distinguished career. He won the overall win title twice and was the first jockey with 500 wins in a season when he won 515 races in 1973. And, as it turns out, this Oshawa, Ontario native is no stranger to the NHL rinks. During the winters, when he was competing and living in California, Hawley would serve as a penalty box official at Los Angeles Kings games to be close to his second favourite sport.

14. Who was the first Canadian golfer to win a PGA tour event?

Al Balding

A. Long before Mike Weir was even a twinkle in his parents eyes, Al Balding of Islington, Ontario, at the time a suburb of Toronto, was raised across the road from a golf course. Of course, he would spend much of his time caddying and trying to sneak in some playing time whenever possible. After World War II he worked a regular job and honed his game, and with the help of a friend who bankrolled him in 1952 went out on the pro tour. For the first couple of years nothing much happened until December 1955, when he won the Mayfair Open in Florida, the first of many wins for Balding, who opened a lot of doors for Canadian golfers.

15. What Canadian music legend was well-known in a certain high-speed sport and was also inducted into a sports hall of fame?

A. Guy Lombardo, the leader of the famous Royal Canadians, was usually touring, but in his spare time excelled in the raceboat scene. He won virtually every award available in his class and was the U.S. champion from 1946–49 and 1955–56. He was rewarded for his excellence by being inducted in the U.S. Speedboat Hall of Fame.

16. What Canadian athlete was named after a brewery?

A. If you guessed the talented Carling Bassett, Canada's tennis darling of the 80s you're absolutely right. The daughter of John H. Bassett — who was an excellent tennis player himself — Carling was a child prodigy at the sport. She won the U.S. under-12 tourney and was the first Canadian to win the prestigious Orange Bowl title. On the major circuit by the age of 15, she amazed everyone by making it to the fourth round of Wimbledon, and in 1984 she made it to the semis of the U.S. Open. By the late 1980s, after representing Canada at the 1988 Olympics (she finished fifth in doubles with Jill Hetherington), other priorities called when she married American tennis player Robert Seguso and started a family. She now lives in Florida and is still involved with the sport.

17. Before Lori Kane started to tear up the links, who was the most dominant Canadian on the ladies circuit?

A. Sandra Post of Oakville, Ontario, was a natural athlete from a young age. There was a time in her teens when she had to choose between golf and figure skating, in which she also excelled. Figure skating's loss was golf's gain as Sandra won just about every amateur tournament available in Canada. In 1968, Post decided to turn pro, and capped off an impressive rookie season by winning the LPGA championship — becoming the first non-American to win a major. In total, Post won eight major LPGA tourneys, including back-to-back Dinah Shore Opens, before retiring from the tour in 1984.

18. What is the Lou Marsh Trophy awarded for?

A. Lou Marsh was a fantastic athlete who excelled in just about every sport he attempted. A terrific sprinter, swimmer, boxer, and Argo lineman, he later went from competitor to sportswriter. His column at the *Toronto Star* was one of the most popular in the country. After he passed away in 1936, the *Star* and Marsh's friends donated a trophy in his name to be given out annually to Canada's Outstanding Athlete of the Year. Winners of this award have included many of the greatest names in Canadian sports, such as Sandy Hawley, Wayne Gretzky, and Bobby Orr.

Brian Budd

19. Which Canadian soccer player displayed his athleticism by winning the Superstars event?

A. Brian Budd didn't just win the world Superstars event once but three times in 1978, 1979, and 1980. This Toronto-born, Vancouver-raised soccer pro who played for such teams as the Vancouver Whitecaps and the Toronto Metros and Blizzard also represented Canada on our national soccer team. In 1981, Budd captained the North American Superstars team that won the World Team event. Also prominent on that North American team was Canadian hockey player Ron Dugay.

20. Who was the first woman to compete against men in Olympic trapshooting?

A. Calgary-born Susan Nattrass became accustomed to firearms at a young age — her father had himself appeared in three world championship events. In 1974, Susan competed in and won her first of six world championships. It was at the 1976 Montreal Olympics that she became the first woman ever to compete against men at that level. She has stayed active in the sport throughout the years and still competes, juggling shooting events with her schedule as the Athletic Director at St. Mary's University in Nova Scotia.

21. Who was Marlene Streit and what was her claim to Canada's sports fame?

A. Marlene Streit was a true Canadian legend in the sport of golf, inspiring many young women to take up this sport to follow in this tiny five-foot tall, terror-of-the-fairways' footsteps. Born and raised in Cereal, Alberta, she was the only player to have won the Canadian, U.S., British, and Australian amateur championships. She won virtually every amateur golf title available in this country and has won numerous international championships on the senior circuit. In 1998, Streit was appointed as the non-playing captain of the World Amateur Golf team.

22. Which Olympic sport has Canada won more total medals in, figure skating or hockey?

A. Canada totally dominated Olympic hockey for more than 30 years after the sports inception at the 1920 Antwerp Games. Since that time, the eastern European and Scandinavian countries have taken over and surpassed us in our Olympic play. In the meantime, Canada has become a leader in the world of figure skating. As a result, Canada's figure skaters have out-medalled our hockey players, with 2 golds, 7 silvers, and 9 bronzes for a total of 18 medals. Our hockey teams have earned 6 golds, 5 silvers, and 2 bronze.

23. What was the claim to fame of the Montreal Olympic Club?

A. The club, which was founded in 1842 by soldiers of the 93rd Highlanders, was the first official track and field organization in Canada. In 1844, the club held an informal local "Olympics" that was reportedly well publicized and received. The event featured such events as rifle shooting, a 365-metre foot race, the standing leap, and throwing a cricket ball for distance. One event that should be noted was a game of lacrosse, a sport the Highlanders had picked up after seeing it played by the local Caughnawago Indians.

24. Who owns the Toronto Rock of the National Lacrosse League?

A. The very successful Toronto Rock are owned by a syndicate of very high profile sports personalities that includes hockey and baseball executives Bill Watters and Paul Beeston, former hockey superstar Bobby Orr, and current NHLers Tie Domi and Brendan Shanahan. The Rock, who played their first game in 1999, have already won the 1999 and 2000 league championships and continue to be the NLL's marquee franchise. They have shared the Air Canada Centre with the Maple Leafs and the Raptors since the beginning of the 2001 season.

25. Has Canada ever won an Olympic medal in the sport of lacrosse?

A. Yes, in fact we've won the gold every time lacrosse has been played in the Olympics. Unfortunately, lacrosse was only an official Olympic sport on two occasions — in the 1904 Games in St. Louis and 1908 Games in London. At St. Louis, the Canadian entry was represented by the Winnipeg Shamrocks, who cruised past the competition to win the gold quite easily. In 1908, in England, our national all-stars beat the champions of Britain to win our second consecutive gold in this soon-to-be-discontinued Olympic sport. During the gold medal match, one of the Canadians broke his stick and was forced to leave until another stick could be found for him. One of the British players graciously offered to withdraw from the game until the Canadian team could come back to full strength. It makes one wonder if such sportsmanship still exists at that level of competition.

26. What sport did Sharif Khan excel at?

A. The family name Khan is synonymous worldwide with the sport of squash. For generations this family has dominated the sport, winning literally scores of international championships. For instance, members of the Khan family have won the prestigious British Open championships 29 times. Sharif was born in Pakistan but in the 1960s settled in the Toronto area, where he remains today. During his career this elite technician of the sport not only won 15 North American championships, but he also won 12 world championships before retiring from competition in 1982. Still active on the masters circuit, he is a squash pro at one of the country's most prestigious fitness centres and is the director of a children's charity that bears his name.

27. What Canadian father and son have set the world of auto racing on its ears?

A. There are perhaps no bigger names in Canadian auto racing than those of Quebec's Jacques Villeneuve and his late father Gilles. The elder Villeneuve was born in 1950, and was attracted to the speed and danger associated with racing from a young age. As a teenager he began his career by racing snowmobiles and Formula Atlantic cars. A daredevil at heart who rode his talent and ambition to many visits to the winner's circle, Gilles jumped up to the F-1 circuit in 1977. He posted six victories, including the Montreal Grand Prix, and in 1978 came in second to his teammate Jody Schecter for the F-1 championship. Gilles was killed in a practice run for the Belgian Grand Prix on May 8, 1982. Canadians mourned this young man's passing, but it wouldn't be long before another Villeneuve came along and treated us with his superb talents.

Jacques Villeneuve has had an extraordinary career, perhaps even surpassing that of his father's. Born in 1971, Jacques was destined to follow in his family's racing footsteps. In 1995, Villeneuve scored a double-victory, winning the Indianapolis 500 and being voted auto racing's Rookie of the Year. In 1997, took the world championship in Formula-1 racing, and was honoured in Canada with both the Lou Marsh Award and Canadian Athlete of the Year — the first race car driver to achieve this honour.

28. Who was "Torchy" Peden?

Torchy Peden,
(on the left)

A. Big William Peden, born in 1906 in Victoria B.C., showed talent in many sports, but in his teens made cycling his sport of choice. While training for the Olympic trials, it became apparent that the six-foot-two, 220-pound athlete was getting too big for his standard 21-pound racing bike, so a modified bike was prepared for Peden. It was while using the new bike that Peden qualified for the 1928 Olympics in Amsterdam. Unfortunately, Peden blew two tires in the Olympic heats and lost his chance for a medal. Peden turned pro shortly after a new sport had developed south of the border: the six-day indoor bicycle race. This event was played out on special tracks, and the racers usually dressed in jockey style clothes, competed in teams of two men. Each team rode in shifts with the goal to complete as many laps as possible in the allotted time. It was a tough way to make a living, but Torchy prospered, his talents vaulting him to a winning percentage of over 25 percent in almost 150 races — a record that would stand until the mid-1960s.

29. What Canadian tennis player was nicknamed "The Hurricane"?

A. "Hurricane" Helen Kelesi has proven throughout her life that she is a true champion. Not only has she achieved great success on the tennis court, but she has shown courage and grace by bouncing back from serious adversity. Helen was born in Victoria, B.C., in 1969. By the time she was a teenager, she had won the Canadian junior championship and had a top-three ranking on the world junior circuit. After turning pro in 1986, she won her first major tournament, the Japanese Open, and knocked off such stars as Helena Sukova and Hana Mandlikova to greatly improve her standing in the world rankings. Along the way she was also able to capture herself four Canadian Opens, and it looked like the future was bright for the pretty Canadian. But when Helen began getting headaches and suffering from blackouts, it became apparent that something was wrong. Medical testing confirmed the worst, as Helen was diagnosed with a large brain tumour. Showing true grit, she bounced back from brain surgery and surprised everyone by making a tennis comeback. Today, Helen is a much-sought-after speaker who shares her life story with dignity and shows the courage and resolve that has always been the Hurricane's trademark.

30. Who was known as "the first woman of Canadian golf"?

A. Ada Mackenzie was a true sports pioneer who not only furthered the game of golf, but was one of the forces that created the opportunities for women to excel in the sport and be accepted athletes.

As a player, Ada Mackenzie was a legend. Learning the game from her father, Mackenzie won her first tournament at the young age of 13. Her career spanned 60 years, and included victories in five Canadian Ladies' Open Amateurs, two Bermuda Opens, ten

Toronto championships, and nine Ontario Ladies' Amateurs. Later, on the seniors circuit, she won the seniors' Canadian title eight times, the last one in 1969 at the age of 78.

Perhaps even more significant than her playing career, though, was Ada Mackenzie's contribution as one of the sport's builders. When visiting England, Mackenzie observed that the game was much more accessible to British women than in Canada. After arriving back home, she went to work raising money and in 1924 opened the Ladies' Golf and Tennis Club of Toronto, the only course in the world at the time to cater almost exclusively to women. (Men were allowed to play as well, though only at certain times.)

Ada Mackenzie

31. What sport is Paul Tracy a champion in?

A. Toronto-born Paul Tracy is one of the most consistent drivers in the sport of cart auto racing. This veteran of the oval
track started his racing career driving go-carts at the age of eight.
A veteran now of ten years on the circuit, Paul's 20 career wins put
him second only to Michael Andretti among active cart drivers.
Among his wins are victories at such major races as Long Beach,
Road America, and Vancouver. Tracy is a married father of two and
now resides in Las Vegas.

32. What world-ranked Canadian race driver was tragically killed in 1999?

A. New Westminster, B.C. native Greg Moore was one of the top
drivers in the cart circuit. In 71 starts he had accumulated
five victories, his first coming at the 1997 Milwaukee Mile at the
age of 22 — making him the youngest driver ever to win a Cart
race. Among his other wins were the 1998 Rio de Janeiro, and the
1998 U.S. 500. On October 31, 1999, Moore lost control of his
Players Mercedes and crashed driver's side first into the retaining
wall. The Canadian star was only 24 years old.

33. Who was known as "the Moaner"?

A. Born in the Beaches section of Toronto, Ted Reeve was an
athlete, coach, and journalist in his long career. As an athlete he was second to none in courage and heart, playing through
serious injuries that would have stopped many a lesser man. The
hero of the 1930 Grey Cup game, he was also an excellent lacrosse
player, playing on three Mann Cup championship teams in 1926,
1928, and 1930. In the late 1920s, he began writing a column for
The Toronto Telegram called "Sporting Extras" as a sideline. His easy
witty manner of writing made his column one of the most popular

in the country. Reeve's celebrity grew to the point that, after serving overseas in World War II, he returned home to a waiting crowd of friends and fans.

34. Who spent his life teaching Canadians the proper road to physical fitness?

A. Lloyd Percival was known for decades as Canada's foremost authority on physical fitness and education. In 1941, he began hosting a CBC radio program called "Sports College," which was really a correspondence school taught over the airwaves. The show had become so popular that at its peak, Percival had 80,000 students registered. Off the airwaves, Percival was one of the most respected track and field coaches in the country. Several of Canada's elite athletes improved their careers through training with Lloyd at his then state-of-the-art Fitness Institute. Percival was inducted into the Canadian Sports Hall of Fame in 1976.

35. What amazing feat did Sharon Wood accomplish on May 20, 1986?

A. Halifax-born and Burnaby-raised Wood became the first North American woman to climb to the 9,848-metre summit of Mount Everest — the world's highest mountain.

From a young age, Wood was fascinated by Canada's west coast mountains and scaled her first local mountain peak at the age of 12. Working as a mountain guide in the Rockies, she honed her skills and, when the opportunity arose, she joined the thirteen-member Canadian team that was planning to tackle Everest. She and her partner Dwayne Congdon braved 100 kilometre an hour winds to climb the last section of the famed mountain tip. On May 20, at roughly 9:00 p.m., two days after her 29th birthday, Sharon Wood was able to stand at the highest point on Earth and look down on the beauty of the world below.

36. What former world champion archer was the pride and joy of Wetaskiwin, Alberta?

A. On August 16, 1969, in Valley Forge, Pennsylvania, Dorothy Lidstone became the first Canadian ever to win the World Archery championships. In winning the title she smashed the world women's record for the event with a total of 2361 points — only 60 short of the men's record. The accomplishment earned him an appearance on *The Garry Moore Show* on U.S. television. She was inducted into the Canadian Sports Hall of Fame in 1977.

37. Can you mix and match these well-known athletes and their equally well-known relatives?

a. Wendel Clark	A. Dave Hilton Jr.
b. Vince Carter	B. Joey Kocur
c. Arturo Gatti	C. George Armstrong
d. Rick Vaive	D. Tracy McGrady

A. **a.** Former Toronto Maple Leaf captain and tough guy Wendel Clark and **B.** former Detroit Red Wing enforcer Joey Kocur are cousins.

b. Toronto Raptors' Vince Carter and **D.** Orlando Magic's Tracy McGrady are distant cousins.

c. Former junior lightweight champion of the world Arturo Gatti and **A.** Dave Hilton Jr., the former WBC world super middleweight champ are brothers-in-law.

d. Former Toronto Maple Leaf Captain Rick Vaive is the nephew of **C.** George Armstrong, a longtime Leaf Captain, coach, and executive.

38. In which sport has Canada won the most total medals in Olympic competition: swimming, rowing, or track and field?

A. According to the Canadian Olympic Association and *The Canadian Global Almanac*, our greatest Olympic success has come in track and field, where Canada has won 13 gold medals, 14 silver, and 23 bronze for a grand total of 50. Swimming comes is second with 38 total medals won with rowing third at 31.

39. Which participation sport or physical activity is most popular with Canadians?

A. According to a 1998 Statistics Canada survey, the most participated in sport in Canada is golf with an estimated 1.8 million people who have on some level or another spent time out on the links. Following close behind at roughly 1.5 million national participants is our old standby hockey, with baseball rounding out the survey at about 1.4 million.

40. What was the Dubin Inquiry?

A. Formed after the Ben Johnson debacle at the 1988 Seoul Olympics, the Canadian government established this inquiry into the use of performance drugs and other banned practices in athletic competition. Appeal Court Chief Justice Charles L. Dubin was appointed to oversee the proceedings and rule on its findings. The inquiry sat for 91 days, and called over 100 witnesses — the star witness being Ben Johnson himself. Dubin's recommendations included more unannounced random testing of athletes, stricter guidelines, and harsh penalties for athletes found to be using performance enhancing drugs. Dubin felt that proper education of young athletes about the dangers of drugs was necessary to combat the growing use of drugs in amateur sport.

41. What Canadians were instrumental in helping form the Canadian Special Olympics?

A. Dr. Frank Hayden, a Toronto-based teacher and researcher, found that it was possible for the mentally disabled to become physically fit and to learn the skills to ably participate in sports. Dr. Hayden's work drew the attention of Eunice Kennedy Shriver (sister of the late John F. Kennedy), a renowned humanitarian. With the help of the Kennedy Foundation, Hayden and Shriver established the Special Olympics in the United States in 1968. To make sure that Canada had a similar event of our own, Dr. Hayden contacted a special friend of his, well-known athlete, broadcaster and humanitarian Harry "Red" Foster. Under Foster's care and guidance the Canadian Special Olympics were born, with the first events held in Toronto in 1969.

Harry "Red" Foster

42. What sport did John Saunders excel in before becoming a high-profile sportscaster?

A. Montreal-raised John Saunders was quite an athlete in his youth. An all-star defenceman, he received a scholarship to play hockey at Western Michigan University from 1974–76. Coming back to Canada, he caught the broadcasting bug and learned his craft at several small radio and TV stations before landing a job at CityTv in Toronto between 1980 and 1982. John then went state-side, where he has since hosted NCAA basketball, college football, and NHL hockey for ABC sports and ESPN.

43. What native of Prince Edward Island has become one of the most dominant forces in the world of ladies golf?

A. Charlottetown's own favourite daughter Lori Kane has become one of the most successful players on the elite LPGA circuit over the past few years. Starting to play the game at the tender age of 5, Kane joined the tour in the mid-90s and, after an amazing nine second-place finishes, she finally broke through in August 2000 when she won the Michelob Light Classic Mizuno Open and the Takefuji Classic. This proud Canadian has won the prestigious Bobbie Rosenfeld Award as Canada's top female athlete on two occasions, in 1997 and 2000, and has earned more than $3 million on the tour.

44. What Canadian has become one of the most consistent players on the PGA tour?

A. Mike Weir, a native of Brights Grove, Ontario, has become one of the most successful golfers in the world today, winning such tournaments as the 1999 Air Canada championship and the 2000 American Express tournament, in which he pocketed a cool $1 million (U.S.) for his victory. What must have made the American Express win even more sweet for Weir was that he defeated the famous Tiger Woods, relegating the golfing legend to runner-up status in this very prestigious championship. In 2000,

Weir became only the seventh player in golf history to earn more than $2.5 million in a season.

45. What Canadian tennis aces won the doubles gold medal at the 2000 Sydney Olympics?

A. It was definitely a busy year for the newly-formed Canadian duo of Daniel Nestor and Sebastian Lareau. After teaming up early in the year, the pair won the Tennis Masters Series Canada tournament in Toronto, and advanced to the quarter finals of the U.S. Open, the French Open, and Wimbledon. But it was at the Olympics later that summer — when they faced the number one team in the world, Australia's Mark Woodforde and Todd Woodbridge — that the underdog Canucks really began to shine. They handed Woodforde and Woodbridge their first loss of the year, and became the first Canadian's to ever win Olympic gold in tennis.

46. Has Canada won more total medals in the Summer or Winter Olympics?

A. This one isn't even close. Since the Olympics' reinvention in 1896 the Summer Olympics have been hands down more successful for Canadians. In total for the 26 Summer Games that we have sent teams to, we have won 53 gold medals, 80 silvers, and 98 bronze for a total of 231 trips to the medal podium. In Canada's 21 visits to the Winter Games, we have won 27 gold medals, 26 silvers, and 30 bronze for a pretty impressive 83 total medals. One thing to keep in mind, though, is that there are many more events in the Summer Games to compete in.

47. In both the Summer and Winter Olympics combined, who's ahead in the Canadian medal count, the guys or the ladies?

A. Before we guys get too smug in our victory, we have to remember that ladies didn't make their first appearance until over 20 years after their male counterparts, and many more events are designed for men than for women. With that in mind, the final tally for men is 201 medals won, against 96 total medals for the ladies. If you want a further breakdown, at the Summer Olympics the men have garnered 157 medals as opposed to the 67 won by females. At the Winter Games, the men also come out on top by a 44–29 total. (Note: these totals don't include combined male-female events such as the ice pairs and ice dance competitions.)

48. Who was Alexandrine Gibb and what was her contribution to Canadian sports?

A. This strong willed and intelligent woman was one of the leaders of a strong women's sports movement that developed in Canada in the 1920s. Born in Toronto in 1892 to an athletically prominent family, Gibb believed that the governing of women's athletics should be in the hands of women, and helped start the Women's Amateur Athletic Federation of Canada. Gibb was instrumental in getting our first Canadian ladies team to compete at the 1928 Olympics, and in recognition of her role she was elected team manager. A popular long-time journalist with *The Toronto Star*, she was the first woman ever appointed to the office of the Ontario Athletic Commission.

49. If golf were to be brought back as an Olympic sport, what country would be considered as the defending champ?

A. Well, if it was anyone other than Canada then it wouldn't have made it into this book, would it? The only time golf was included in the Olympic itinerary was in 1904 when the Games were held in St. Louis, Missouri. Though a total of 87 golfers participated and 32 of those qualified, it turned out to be a two-player race between U.S. amateur champion H. Chandler Egan and forty-six-year-old George S. Lyon of Toronto. The Canadian was playing some of the best golf of his life, shooting a course record 77 in the finals, and stood victorious — and celebrated with a long, uninterrupted walk through the clubhouse on his hands. An interesting side note is that Lyon had, up to that time, only been playing golf for eight years, picking up a club for the first time at the advanced age of 38.

50. What did Canada fail to do at both Olympic Games we have hosted — the 1976 Montreal Summer Games and the 1988 Calgary Winter Games?

A. Nobody can complain that Canada wasn't a generous host in either of the Games. In fact, we may have been too hospitable, for we left all the gold medals for our guests and didn't take any ourselves. Greg Joy in 1976, and Elizabeth Manley and Brian Orser in 1988 came closest with silver medal wins, but we were never able to get to that gold medal podium.

51. Cathy Townsend of Montreal, Quebec, became the first Canadian woman to win a world championship in what sport?

A. This little lady traveled all the way to the Philippines in 1975 to win the prestigious World Cup of Bowling. Many of her belongings and equipment were lost upon arriving in Manila, and rushing to replace them really cut into her practice time. But even with those obstacles, she proved to be the cream among the 27 nation field, defeating Hattianne Morissette of Bermuda to bring the title to Canada for the first time.

52. Since the mid-1990s, which Canadian has dominated the competition in the world of professional squash?

A. Introduced to the sport at the age of eight by his father, himself a top-rated over-40s champion, Jonathan Power has been squash's most-exciting player since joining the Professional Squash Association tour in 1991. Power, born in Comox, B.C., and based in Toronto, won his first tournament title in Chicago in 1992, and has continued winning ever since, taking more than 20 PSA titles and topping the world rankings for most of the time since the mid-90s. The colourful and out-spoken Powers is one of the finest athletes in the world today, and will continue to be a force in the world of squash for some years to come.

53. What sport is the game of baggataway better known as?

A. First played by native Canadians, baggataway was called "lacrosse" by the French settlers who first witnessed the aboriginal sport in the 1700s. The French adopted a less violent set of rules, and the sport soon became a popular pastime with the new Canadians. By the late 19th and early 20th century, lacrosse was our most popular sport, and Canadian teams dominated in international play. In fact, in the only two times that lacrosse was included as an Olympic sport, in 1904 and 1908, Canada came away with gold medals.

54. Was Canada ever cursed against winning a world championship?

A. It happened at the World Cup of Curling championships held in Germany in 1972. In the tenth end of the gold medal match between the U.S. and Canada, it appeared that the Americans had just made the game-winning shot when team member Bob LaBonte fell down, accidentally moving a Canadian stone in the process. The error allowed us to tie the game and then win it in an extra end. It was at that time that LaBonte delivered a hex that he said would prevent Canada from ever winning a world curling title again. And wouldn't you know it, it would be eight long years before Canada would again be crowned as the sport's champions. Fortunately the effects of the curse quickly evaporated after that, and Canada has since won 21 world titles.

55. What connection does Canadian music icon Neil Young have with Canadian sports?

A. This proud Canuck was born in Toronto in 1945 to Edna and Scott Young. While Edna was a former Canadian TV game show personality, Scott was a prominent author and sports writer. Along with covering sports for some of the most prestigious dailies in the country, the elder Young also wrote biographies of Foster Hewitt and Punch Imlach, and sports books for children, such as A Boy at the Leafs Camp and the Hockey Heroes series. It's said that Neil's seventies classic "Old Man" was written in tribute to his dad.

56. What Canadian gymnastics star is now a successful gymnastics commentator with NBC?

A. Etobicoke-born Elfi Schlegel was a gymnastics prodigy from a young age. Victorious in many national and international junior tournaments, she moved south after high school to attend the University of Florida. Before her graduation in 1986 with a degree in telecommunications, she set the NCAA on fire with 12 NCAA Southeast Region tourney wins (the best total in region history) and was a six-time All-American. The winner of the all-around gymnastics gold medal at the 1978 Commonwealth

Games, she was considered one of the gold favourites going into the 1980 Moscow Olympics. Unfortunately, the boycott of those Games by most Western nations in protest of the Soviet invasion of Afghanistan put her dream on ice. In 1988, Elfi got her start in front of the cameras, covering the sport on CBC during the 1988 Seoul Games. She proved to be a natural, and since 1992 has covered the sport with NBC.

Louis Cyr

57. What world record did Canadian Victor Delamarre set over seventy-five years ago?

A. With a height of just 5'6" and a weight of roughly 150 pounds, Delamarre's small frame didn't hint at the great strength he possessed. Victor, who was born in 1888 in the Lac St. Jean region of Quebec, astounded people with his feats of strength and dreamed that someday he would have the fame of his hero, the great Louis Cyr. During one of his displays of strength, Delamarre set a record that would last for years to come by lifting 309.5 pounds with only one hand. He was also known to lift human platforms weighing as much as 7,000 pounds and carry vehicles strapped to his back up ladders. In 1931, to help support his family during the Depression, he began a successful new career as a professional wrestler.

58. Who was the first Canadian to be named as the North American Soccer League's Player of the Year?

A. In 1978, twenty-three-year-old Bob Lenarduzzi received the prestigious honour while a star player for the Vancouver Whitecaps. This Vancouver-born defence player had star written all over him from a young age when he went to England to play for English Fourth Division team FC Reading at the tender age of 15. After a five year stint there, it was back to Canada where, as a member of the Whitecaps he also played as part of the Canadian team at the 1984 Olympics. Turning to coaching with the Canadian Soccer League's Vancouver 86ers, he eventually earned himself a lengthy stint as head coach of the Canadian National and Olympic teams.

59. What ladies' team sport has our Canadian Paralympics won three consecutive gold medals in?

A. The ladies have been dominant in the sport of wheelchair basketball for the past decade and a half. Starting with a silver medal at the 1986 Pan-Am Games and a fourth place finish at the 1988 Seoul Paralympics, Canada's fortunes in the sport have risen dramatically at the world level. Our national team has won titles in the 1994 and 1998 Gold Cup championships and gold medals at the prestigious Qualification of the Americas tournament in 1998 and 1999. Even with all these victories under their belts, there can be no doubt that their greatest achievements have been the gold medal victories at the 1992, 1996, and 2000 Paralympic Games.

Terry Fox

60. Which athletic figure is generally considered to be Canada's greatest hero?

A. On April 12, 1980, in Newfoundland, a young man dipped his prosthetic leg into the Atlantic Ocean and began what he called the Marathon of Hope. A few years earlier, Terry Fox had lost his leg to osteogenic sarcoma, a rare form of bone cancer, and while recovering planned this run across the country to raise money for and awareness of cancer. More than 5,000 kilometres later, near Thunder Bay, Ontario, Terry fell ill and it was discovered that the cancer had returned — this time in his lungs. No Canadian can ever forget the grief of the nation when Terry succumbed to the disease on June 28, 1981. But the Marathon of Hope was just beginning, for after Terry's passing, Canadians have joined together to continue Terry's dream, raising millions of dollars in the hope of finding a cure for this killer disease.

61. Which great Canadian from years past was known as the World's Strongest Man?

A. Montreal-born Louis Cyr astounded the world with demonstrations of his enormous power at a time before accurate official records were kept. Some of the public feats that he became known for were incredible. One published report said that in England on January 19, 1889, in front of a crowd of 5,000 — including the Prince of Wales — Cyr performed three amazing lifts: he raised 4,100 pounds stretched across his back; lifted a 314 pound barrel of cement to his shoulder with one hand; and lifted a 551-pound weight with one finger.

62. What was Doug Hepburn's claim to Canadian sport's fame?

A. The inspiring Hepburn was no stranger to adversity, having been born cross-eyed and with a club foot. Surgery to correct the foot left his leg withered, but that didn't stop this powerhouse from winning the 1953 World Weightlifting championship, or from being awarded the Lou Marsh Trophy that year as Canada's Top Athlete. The following year Hepburn continued his success, smashing most existing records at the 1954 British Empire Games. The success came despite the fact that he was entirely self-taught.

Doug Heburn

BIBLIOGRAPHY

Canadian Football League. *Canadian Football League Facts, Figures and Record Book*. Triumph Books, 2000

Conner, Brendan; Russell, Nancy. *Slam Dunk: the Raptors and the NBA*. Scarborough: Prentice Hall Canada Inc., 1995

Diamond, Dan. *Hockey Hall of Fame: The Official Registry of the Game's Honour Roll*. Toronto: Doubleday Canada Limited, 1996

Diamond, Dan. *Total Hockey*. Kingston: Total Sports Publishing Inc., 2000

Heller, Bill with Ron Turcotte. *The Will to Win: Ron Turcotte's Ride to Glory*. Saskatoon: Fifth House Publishers, 1992

LeBlanc, Michael, L. *Hotdogs, Heroes & Hooligans: The Story of Baseball's Major League Teams*. Detroit: Visible Ink Press, 1994

Long, Wendy. *Celebrating Excellence: Canadian Women Athletes*. Vancouver: Polestar 1995

Lumley, Elizabeth. *Canadian Who's Who 2000 Millennial Edition*. Toronto: University of Toronto Press, 2000.

McFarlane, Brain. *It Happened in Baseball: Amazing Tales from the Fields of Dreams*. Toronto: Stoddart Publishing, 1993

McFarlane, Brain. *It Happened in Hockey: Weird and Wonderful Stories from Canada's Greatest Game*. Toronto: Stoddart Publishing, 1991

Morrison, Michael; Brown, Gerry. 2001 ESPN *Information Please Sports Almanac*. Hyperion, 2000.

Ray, Randy; Kearney, Mark. *The Great Canadian Book of Lists*. Toronto: Hounslow Press, 1999

Ray, Randy; Kearney, Mark. *The Great Canadian Trivia Book* 1. Toronto: Hounslow Press, 1996

Ray, Randy; Kearney, Mark. *The Great Canadian Trivia Book* 2. Toronto: Hounslow Press, 1998

Sports Illustrated 2000 *Sports Almanac*. Boston: Little Brown 1999.

The Baseball Encyclopedia. New York: MacMillan Publishing.

Wise, S.F.; Fisher, Douglas. *Canada's Sporting Heroes*. Don Mills, ON: General Publishing Co., 1974

Young, Mark. Ed. *Guinness Book of Sports Records: Winners and Champions*. New York: Sterling Publishing Co.

ABOUT THE AUTHOR

Sportswriter and broadcaster Eddie Zawadzki is quickly becoming a familiar face and voice in the world of professional kickboxing and amateur boxing.

As a promoter, he has organized many successful events, featuring such notable stars as Muhammed Ali, George Chuvalo, Floyd Patterson, and Don Cherry, to name a few. He has promoted live boxing shows featuring such Canadian stars as the Hilton Bros., and Billy "The Kid" Irwin, as well as closed circuit broadcasts of several world championship bouts.

Over the past number of years, he has handled publicity for over a dozen world championship kickboxing fights, and has promoted several provincial and international amateur boxing shows.

Zawadzki also handled publicity for a Canadian concert venue that featured such headliners as The Tragically Hip, Colin James, The Doobie Brothers, and Waylon Jennings.

Born and raised in Toronto, Zawadzki was a fine multi-sport athlete and has always been active in charities. He has served as sports editor of *The Toronto Free Press*, and has had articles in such papers as *The Toronto Sun*. A few years ago, he stepped in front of the camera as a colour commentator, and has appeared as a fight analyst on TSN, CBC, and Rogers Television.